Mark Twain

T0345541

Titles in the series Critical Lives present the work of leading cultural figures of the modern period. Each book explores the life of the artist, writer, philosopher or architect in question and relates it to their major works.

In the same series

Mark Twain

Kevin J. Hayes

REAKTION BOOKS

For Nancy Hayes

Published by Reaktion Books Ltd
Unit 32, Waterside
44–48 Wharf Road
London N1 7UX, UK
www.reaktionbooks.co.uk

First published 2018

Copyright © Kevin J. Hayes 2018

All rights reserved

No part of this publication may be reproduced, stored in a retrieval system,
or transmitted, in any form or by any means, electronic, mechanical,
photocopying, recording or otherwise, without the prior permission
of the publishers

Printed and bound in Great Britain by Bell & Bain, Glasgow

A catalogue record for this book is available from the British Library

ISBN 978 1 78023 974 3

Contents

Mark Twain, carte de visite, 1883.

Introduction

Listing the hundred books that influenced him most, Henry Miller put Mark Twain's *Adventures of Huckleberry Finn* among such novels as Thomas Mann's *The Magic Mountain* and Louis-Ferdinand Céline's *Journey to the End of the Night*. Miller, who fondly remembered both *Huckleberry Finn* and *The Adventures of Tom Sawyer* from his youth, longed to reread them as he wrote *The Books in My Life*. Though he appreciated their author, Miller nonetheless associated Twain's writings with children's books. On his European travels he happened to discuss American literature with some Greek enthusiasts. Playing the provocateur, Miller called Walt Whitman the only great writer the United States had ever produced. One listener wondered whether Twain deserved recognition as a great writer. No, Miller replied, Twain is for adolescents.[1]

Miller's most startling discussion of Twain occurs in *The Time of the Assassins*. Noticing that in 1884, the same year *Huckleberry Finn* appeared, French novelist Joris-Karl Huysmans published *Against the Grain*, Miller said that while Twain was using his 'quaint, piquant Americanese' to create a classic of literary realism, Huysmans left realism and naturalism behind to create a masterpiece of decadence with a modern sensibility. Huck Finn journeys down the Mississippi; Huysmans' hero journeys into the self, into the world of imagination and intellect.[2]

Other twentieth-century authors spoke about Twain's masterpiece with awe. In *The Smart Set*, an early modernist magazine, H. L.

Mencken frequently championed Twain's works, remarking at one point, 'Nothing has ever been written in America to surpass *Huckleberry Finn*. It is rather more than a mere book; it is almost a whole literature.' Ernest Hemingway famously asserted that all modern American literature comes from *Huckleberry Finn*. Some may quibble with this assertion, but Twain adumbrated Hemingway's fundamental theory of composition when he observed, 'A successful book is not made of what is *in* it, but of what is left *out* of it.'[3]

Despite the level of respect Mencken and Hemingway held, Miller's ambivalence may more accurately reflect the attitude toward Twain among modernist authors. Associating his works with boys' books, Miller ignored Twain's travel writing. Together, *Innocents Abroad*, *Roughing It* and *Life on the Mississippi* form a body of work sufficient to establish Mark Twain as a major voice in American literature. Miller's emphasis on Twain's fiction shows how the novel had come to dominate all other literary genres by the twentieth century.[4]

Few authors since Twain can deny his importance to literary history, no matter how few are willing to acknowledge his influence. His most enthusiastic readers have still found flaws in his work. Hemingway thought that *Huckleberry Finn* falls apart in the end. Leonard Woolf agreed, believing the elaborate humour late in the novel was far too protracted. Jorge-Luis Borges found its final third downright annoying. Though he considered *Huckleberry Finn* a great book, he disliked one major character: Tom Sawyer. Tom's silly jokes spoil the novel's later chapters.[5]

The greatness of *Huckleberry Finn* has cast Twain's other writings in shadow. In *Our America*, a cultural critique written the decade after Twain's death, Waldo Frank observed, 'Out of the bitter wreckage of his long life, one great work emerges by whose contrasting fire we can observe the darkness.' Frank may overstate the case, but his words have had an impact. Charlie Chaplin, for one, took to heart what Frank had to say. When an interviewer mentioned Mark Twain, Chaplin replied, 'Ah, now you're getting me back on my favorite topic.' He did not dwell on Twain in the interview but brought up Frank's interpretation, which Chaplin considered 'a profound, penetrating analysis of the man'. Chaplin's own career demonstrates how Twain's work has affected those after him. In essence Chaplin faced the same dilemma Twain had faced: how to be a funny man yet make one's work transcend its humour and embody the soul of its creator.[6]

Following Waldo Frank, T. S. Eliot called *Huckleberry Finn* Twain's only masterpiece, but what a masterpiece! Eliot placed Huck Finn in the upper echelon of fictional characters, ranking him with such predecessors as Ulysses, Hamlet and Faust. He also refuted those who critiqued the book's later chapters. Eliot appreciated the cyclical structure, how the mood of its ending brings Huck's story back to its beginning.[7]

When Kenneth Rexroth revisited *Huckleberry Finn* in a regular column he contributed to the *Saturday Review* during the 1960s, he found the novel a turning point in literary history, a challenge to the past and an anticipation of the future. The way he characterizes Twain's masterpiece makes it resemble Huysmans' *Against the Grain*. *Huckleberry Finn*, according to Rexroth, portrays two comrades drifting past civilization, 'a civilization hostile, haunted, valueless, and early decadent'.[8]

Whereas Eliot associated Huck with Ulysses, Rexroth viewed *Huckleberry Finn* as a kind of anti-*Odyssey*. Odysseus battles Poseidon, but Huck and Jim cooperate with the Mississippi; either that or yield to it passively. Each episode of Homer's *Odyssey* is a triumph of reason; each episode of Huck's odyssey offers another perspective into a universe of moral chaos in a manner that foreshadows William Butler Yeats's apocalyptic poem 'The Second Coming'. Rexroth also refuted those who have disliked the book's later portions. The ending of *Huckleberry Finn* sounded to Rexroth like something from Samuel Beckett. Huck and Jim are recaptured by the world from which they had fled, and the novel shades into 'Black Comedy, into the theater of cruelty'.[9]

The *Huckleberry Finn* centenary prompted many to reread and reconsider Twain's masterpiece. Norman Mailer, for one, tested Hemingway's theory, wondering whether all modern American literature really came from *Huckleberry Finn*. Mailer saw the book's general influence on John Dos Passos, Sinclair Lewis and John Steinbeck and identified some specific modern works among its literary progeny. Earlier Waldo Frank had recognized 'more than a superficial kinship' between *Huckleberry Finn* and Sherwood Anderson's first novel, *Windy McPherson's Son*. Mailer added to the list of *Huckleberry Finn*'s kin: J. D. Salinger's *Catcher in the Rye*, Saul Bellow's *Adventures of Augie March* and James Dickey's *Deliverance*. Like Twain before them, two additional twentieth-century American authors – Kurt Vonnegut and Joseph Heller – have understood how resilient irony can be. And William Faulkner, to use Mailer's final example, achieved a similar tone when he chose a similar theme: maniacal men feuding in deep swamps.[10]

Though none of Twain's other works have had as great an impact as *Huckleberry Finn* on the literature to come, several have resonated with modern readers and writers. The title of *The Gilded Age*, the novel Twain co-wrote with Charles Dudley Warner, now serves to label the late nineteenth century. George Orwell challenged the idea that *Tom Sawyer* and *Huckleberry Finn* were boys' books but argued that Twain's travel writings, especially *Roughing It* and *Life on the Mississippi*, represent his best work.[11]

Life on the Mississippi has defined the river for many readers. Harriet Monroe said that Twain's book put the Mississippi 'on the map of art even as the *Iliad* placed Troy there, and *Don Quixote* Spain'. Simone de Beauvoir enjoyed reading *Life on the Mississippi* while on a bus ride to New Orleans in the 1950s. Twain's book gave her a better view of the Mississippi than her bus window:

the massive levees erected along the lower Mississippi since Twain's day have obscured the view of the river from the highway.[12]

Other works have appealed to Twain's fellow authors. A. E. Housman, though quite fond of *Huckleberry Finn*, also knew such minor works as *A Tramp Abroad* and *Tom Sawyer Abroad*. Housman used to pull *A Tramp Abroad* down from the shelf and read its funniest chapters to lift his spirits. *A Connecticut Yankee in King Arthur's Court* has been interpreted as a harbinger of the destructive technology that would manifest itself during the twentieth century. And John Cleese quoted *Following the Equator*, Twain's account of his round-the-world lecture tour, to illustrate a persistent American paradox: the impulse to conform in a land of freedom.[13]

'After an author has been dead for some time,' the American humorist Robert Benchley quipped, 'it becomes increasingly difficult for his publishers to get out a new book by him each year.' When Mark Twain died in 1910, he left his complete *Autobiography* unpublished, suggesting it remain so for a hundred years. Harper & Brothers, the publishing firm that had taken control of his work, could not wait that long and issued an abridged version in 1924. Roughly organized the way its author intended, this edition relates the details of Twain's life not as they had occurred chronologically but as they occur to him in recollection. It is comprised of rants and reminiscences Twain dictated to a stenographer during his final decade. Leonard Woolf found the work 'a disorderly, untidy, ramshackle book', but one revealing 'a broad vein of common sense streaked by genius'. Using a version of free association, Twain's innovative structure parallels contemporary psychological thought. Not everyone liked the approach. Benchley spoofed Twain's structure, creating a mock autobiography on the same pattern.[14]

Some readers have seen modernist qualities in Twain's *Autobiography*. It begged comparison with James Joyce's *Ulysses*, which had appeared two years earlier. The comparison was not necessarily positive. Richard Aldington argued that both Twain and Joyce satirized people to degrade them, not to help them improve and excel. Making another modernist comparison, Aldington suggested that people in the post-Dada era could find in Twain's work 'a new aesthetic shudder and cause for tittering paradoxes'.[15]

Parts of Twain's autobiography left unpublished in 1924 appeared in 1940 as *Mark Twain in Eruption*, an edition prepared by Bernard DeVoto. And in 1959 Charles Neider included additional unpublished passages in his edition of the *Autobiography*, which eschews Twain's innovative organization by rearranging its material chronologically. Hemingway had copies of both DeVoto and Neider in his library: further testament to his ongoing passion for Mark Twain.[16]

When Neider's edition appeared, approximately one-third of Twain's manuscript material remained unpublished. The editors at the Mark Twain Project respected his wishes in regard to the complete *Autobiography*, withholding its publication until 2010. They restored Twain's original organization and included the previously unpublished material. One recent reader has felt in Twain's autobiography 'the raw energy of Ernest Hemingway'. Others have had more difficulty with the work. Reviewing the new edition, Garrison Keillor called it a 'dreary meander of a memoir'.[17]

At its best Twain's autobiography applies techniques he had begun using in his earliest published fiction, techniques associated with the humorists of the Old Southwest. In an episode dating from when he worked as a printer's apprentice, for instance, Twain remembers when his boss meted out punishment by confining him to the upstairs print shop. The punishment is not too hard to take: while biding his time he eats a whole watermelon. For Twain, a watermelon from the American South was akin to ambrosia. As he says in *Pudd'nhead Wilson*, 'It was not a Southern watermelon that Eve took; we know it because she repented.'[18]

Beset by boredom upon finishing the watermelon, Twain seeks a creative way to dispose of the rind. His little brother Henry happens to walk past, so he drops the shell of the watermelon on him, scoring a direct hit:

> That shell smashed down right on the top of his head and drove him into the earth up to the chin. The chunks of that broken melon flew in every direction like a spray, and they broke third story windows all around. They had to get a jack such as they hoist buildings with to pull him out.[19]

These dynamic words are those of a natural-born storyteller filtered through the tall talk that was a vital part of the tales Mark Twain heard and read in his youth.

Though the watermelon episode reinforces Twain's gift for storytelling, it presents a problem when read as autobiography. How can biographical fact be sifted from Twain's tall talk? Read by itself, the watermelon episode is an obvious fabrication. Read with his other books, it sounds strangely familiar. In *Roughing It* Twain recalls dropping a whole watermelon from an upstairs window onto his friend John. Clearly Twain shaped his personal stories to suit the circumstances, freely changing details and substituting characters as necessary. In his supposedly non-fictional works, to use Twain's own words against him, 'Truth is more of a stranger than fiction.'[20]

Sometimes Twain fesses up to his fibs. In another episode from *Roughing It,* he presents in direct discourse something he supposedly said to a desperado. After enclosing his speech in quotation marks, Twain admits, 'If I did not really say that to him I at least felt a sort of itching desire to do it.'[21] With his admission, we readers learn that we have been duped, but because Twain admits his fiction so quickly we cannot get too upset at being led astray. We might even empathize with him: we have all imagined witty retorts in retrospect.

Subtler episodes in Twain's autobiography make separating fact from fiction more difficult. Writing under a pseudonym, he claimed the right to fictionalize his life however he saw fit. Many personal stories Twain tells, though wildly exaggerated, are nonetheless based on fact. To supplement his autobiographical writings, previously unknown essays and interviews from people who knew him personally, heard him speak or read his works continue to surface. To be sure, every biography is but an approximation of its subject's life. Twain himself said as much: 'Biographies are but the clothes and buttons of the man – the biography of the man himself cannot be written.'[22] Despite its inherent difficulties, biography writing remains a worthy endeavour. Now is the time to synthesize the new information and retell the story of Mark Twain's life afresh.

1

The Old Southwest

Visible on clear nights for the preceding month, Halley's Comet reached its perihelion on 16 November 1835. Two weeks later, on 30 November, in Monroe County, Missouri, in 'the almost invisible village of Florida' John Marshall Clemens and his wife Jane welcomed their sixth infant to this world. They named him Samuel Langhorne Clemens but called him Sam. From 1863 he would call himself 'Mark Twain'. In the early twentieth century a local historian would call his birth 'an event of historical importance to the whole nation and by far the biggest event in the history of Monroe County'.[1]

Sam Clemens liked to say he came in with Halley's Comet, but a down-to-earth coincidence may be more pertinent to his literary life. The year Sam was born Augustus Baldwin Longstreet published *Georgia Scenes*. Longstreet's collection of tales and sketches is the leading work in the literary history of the Old Southwest, a loosely defined region stretching from the Georgia pines to the Mississippi valley that gave rise to a unique brand of humour. Clemens started writing for publication before he left his teens, and his early work shows an unmistakable affinity to the humorists of the Old Southwest.

The Clemens family reached Missouri in a roundabout way, the same way many contemporary families reached the Old Southwest.[2] The story of Marshall Clemens is the story of countless other men growing up in the South during the early nineteenth century, the story of a man on a peripatetic journey in search of the main chance. Though his family had deteriorated by the time of his birth in 1798,

Marshall Clemens would boast about its Virginia roots, claiming to belong to the FFV, the First Families of Virginia. Mark Twain says in *Roughing It* that his father left him 'a sumptuous legacy of pride in his fine Virginian stock'. And in *Puddin'head Wilson* he reiterates: 'In Missouri a recognized superiority attached to any person who hailed from Old Virginia; and this superiority was exalted to supremacy when a person of such nativity could also prove descent from the First Families of that great commonwealth.'[3]

After Marshall's birth, his mother bore four more children before her husband perished in a house-raising accident. Widow Clemens and her brood left Virginia for Kentucky, where Marshall read law, earned a licence to practise and met Jane Lampton, a vibrant young woman with fiery red hair who had promised herself to a medical student. To spite her beau after an argument, Jane impulsively married Marshall Clemens. They were an odd couple, her sense of humour and obvious intelligence contrasting with his dour outlook on life.[4]

Once married, the Clemenses moved to Gainesboro, Tennessee, where Jane gave birth to their first son, whom they named Orion after the mythical huntsman. They pronounced his name 'Or-eon' to downplay any pagan associations. Marshall soon moved his family 50 miles east to Jamestown, Tennessee, a town where people were 'as ignorant of the outside world and as unconscious of it as were the other wild animals that inhabited the forest'.[5] Marshall Clemens purchased a 75,000-acre tract near Jamestown as security for his children, but all it gave them was disappointment and dissension.

With a lucklessness to match his restlessness, Marshall found little employment as a lawyer and turned shopkeeper to support his growing family. Jane gave birth to four more children in Tennessee, though only Pamela would survive into adulthood. The Clemenses relocated to Three Forks of Wolf River, where Marshall acquired 200 acres of farmland and built a log cabin. He had a tough go as a farmer and subsequently opened a store at nearby Pall Mall, Tennessee, where he also served as postmaster.[6]

Dissatisfied with his situation, Marshall Clemens welcomed an offer from Jane's brother-in-law John Quarles, who invited them to relocate to Florida, Missouri, a newly established village 150 miles northwest of St Louis. Quarles spoke so highly of the place he convinced Marshall Clemens to sell his store, pack up his family and head for Missouri (pronounced: Missoura). Sam was conceived somewhere between the Wolf and the Mississippi.

Florida was a rough-hewn frontier village containing only twenty houses, log cabins mostly. Practically everyone in town patronized Quarles's general store on Main Street. In old age Twain could still picture its contents: needles, thread, bolts of calico, long-handled tools for home and garden – axes, brooms, rakes, shovels – all displayed wherever they would fit. He also remembered the foodstuffs: wheels of cheese and barrels of everything – salt mackerel, corn whiskey, New Orleans sugar. Whenever the children bought something, they could sample the sugar; whenever their fathers bought something, they could sample the whiskey.[7] Quarles offered Marshall Clemens a partnership in the store and encouraged him to resume his law practice. Three miles from town Quarles owned a large farm and thirty slaves to work it.

The Clemens family moved into a two-room clapboard house on South Mill Street about a hundred feet from Quarles's store. Born two months premature, Sam was a frail little boy – 'sickly and precarious and tiresome and uncertain', in his words – but he grew into a robust lad. A neighbour lady who claimed to be present the night Sam was born said he developed into a healthy, athletic boy: 'If he had not succeeded as a humorist he could certainly have made his fortune as an acrobat.' Years later Sam asked his mother how she felt about him when he was a sickly child. She replied, 'At first I was afraid you would die . . . and after that I was afraid you wouldn't.'[8]

Given his icy demeanour, Marshall Clemens had little influence on Sam, whose temperament was governed by his mother's spirit. His sense of humour came from her, as he admitted: 'She was very bright, and was fond of banter and playful duels of wit; and she had a sort of ability . . . to say a humorous thing with the perfect air of not knowing it to be humorous.'[9] Mark Twain would adopt his mother's deadpan manner when he became a platform lecturer. In 'How to Tell a Story', he explains: 'The humorous story is told gravely; the teller does his best to conceal the fact that he even dimly suspects that there is anything funny about it.'[10]

The family continued to grow – Jane gave birth to Henry in 1838 – but Marshall Clemens's career proved as frustrating in Florida as it had in Jamestown. In 1839 they left Monroe County for Marion, the adjacent county to the northeast, and settled in Hannibal. Despite the move, Florida would remain important to Sam's personal and intellectual development. Until he was eleven or twelve, he spent his summers at the Quarles farm, where summers meant suppers of barbecue, roasting ears and watermelon. The Quarles farm left an enduring impact: it would inspire the Phelps farm in *Huckleberry Finn*. In his autobiography Twain makes it seem idyllic:

> The life which I led there with my cousins was full of charm, and so is the memory of it yet. I can call back the solemn twilight and mystery of the deep woods, the earthy smells, the faint odors of the wild flowers, the sheen of rain-washed foliage, the rattling clatter of drops when the wind shook the trees, the far-off hammering of wood-peckers and the muffled drumming of wood-pheasants in the remoteness of the forest, the snap-shot glimpses of disturbed wild creatures skurrying through the grass, – I can call it all back and make it as real as it ever was, and as blessed.[11]

Sam was closest in age to his cousin Tabitha, who remembered him as mischievous, but lovable: 'He could play more pranks and

E. B. Lasley and C. M. Lasley, *Birthplace of Mark Twain, Florida, Missouri,* photographic print, *c.* 1890.

escape with less punishment than any boy I ever knew. He was always so frank and good-natured that everybody liked him.' Sam was also friends with Uncle John's slaves. He fondly remembered their raccoon and 'possum hunts. Uncle Dan'l, 'whose sympathies were wide and warm and whose heart was honest and simple and knew no guile', was the real-life inspiration for Jim in *Huckleberry Finn*.[12]

Uncle Dan'l influenced Twain's manner of storytelling, as well. On special evenings in Uncle Dan'l's big kitchen Sam would gather with his cousins and the slave children, all grouped together 'with the firelight playing on their faces and the shadows flickering upon the walls, clear back toward the cavernous gloom of the rear'.[13] The children were always eager to hear Uncle Dan'l's stories. One impressed Sam more than any other, a startle story known as 'The Golden Arm'. This traditional African American story had already influenced American literature. Edgar Allan Poe had used a variation to conclude 'Berenice'.[14]

Jnst. Arnst & Co., *Hannibal, Missouri*, lithograph, from Henry Lewis, *Das Illustrirte Mississippithal* (1857), facing p. 268.

After becoming a platform lecturer, Twain added 'The Golden Arm' to his repertoire. He retold it in 'How to Tell a Story' to illustrate the rhetorical pause, 'a dainty thing, and delicate, and also uncertain and treacherous; for it must be exactly the right length – no more and no less – or it fails of its purpose and makes trouble'. As Uncle Dan'l told 'The Golden Arm', the pause came right before the 'snapper' at the story's end.[15]

Once upon a time, Uncle Dan'l would begin, a man married a woman with an arm of pure gold. They lived together on the prairie. After she died and was buried, he could hardly stop thinking about her precious arm, so he dug her up and stole it. Her spirit rose from the grave and, coming closer and closer, repeatedly asked, 'Who's got my golden arm?' Upon conveying the woman's question for a final time in a plaintive and accusatory manner, Uncle Dan'l would then pause. Applying what he learned while listening to Uncle Dan'l, Twain taught others how to finish telling the tale:

Stare steadily and impressively into the face of the farthest-gone auditor – a girl, preferably – and let that awe-inspiring pause begin to build itself in the deep hush. When it has reached exactly the right length, jump suddenly at that girl and yell, '*You've* got it!'

On those hot summer nights, Uncle Dan'l would end the evening with 'The Golden Arm'. As Sam sensed the story approaching, he would feel joy mixed with sadness: once Uncle Dan'l finished 'The Golden Arm', nothing more would separate Sam from bedtime.[16]

Though Uncle John's farm was important to the making of Mark Twain, no place was more important than Hannibal, Missouri, the real-life equivalent of St Petersburg, Tom Sawyer's hometown. Long before writing *The Adventures of Tom Sawyer*, Clemens began making literary use of Hannibal. In an 1852 story, he contrasted its present state with what it was like in 1839, the year his family moved there. What was now a 'flourishing young city' thirteen years earlier had been nothing more than a 'wood-yard', that is, a stopping place for passing steamboats to refuel.[17] Since Sam turned four the year they moved there, he had little memory of Hannibal's early appearance and misrepresents it in retrospect. Originally laid out as a town in 1819, Hannibal was chartered as a city in 1839.

The town's natural features meant more to the Hannibal boys than its manmade ones. Two miles north Holliday's Hill rises nearly three hundred feet above the Mississippi River. Named for Richard and Millicent Holliday, whose mansion on the hill was the finest home in the Hannibal area, Holliday's Hill would become Cardiff Hill in *Tom Sawyer*. Cardiff Hill is just far enough from town 'to seem a Delectable Land, dreamy, reposeful and inviting'. Twain's words recall the Delectable Mountains in John Bunyan's *Pilgrim's Progress*, a book, as Huck Finn says, 'about a man that left his family, it didn't say why'.[18] In real life Richard Holliday left his wife for the California Gold Rush and never returned. Millicent Holliday befriended Jane

Clemens and took an interest in her children. She would be the model for Widow Douglas in *Tom Sawyer* and *Huckleberry Finn*.

McDowell's Cave, a vast limestone cave 2 miles south, would become McDougall's Cave in *Tom Sawyer.* Sam and his friends loved to explore the cave's deep recesses, discovering new tunnels no one had ever entered. Even before writing *Tom Sawyer*, Twain would recall 'its lofty passages, its silence and solitude, its shrouding gloom, its sepulchral echoes, its flitting lights, and more than all, its sudden revelations of branching crevices and corridors where we least expected them'.[19] Together the hill and the cave offered the boys contrasting experiences. Depending on their mood, they could either climb into the sky or descend into the depths of the earth.

Given their distance from town, Holliday's Hill and McDowell's Cave took some effort to reach, but there was another natural feature that was always nearby: the Mississippi River. Swimming, fishing, boating, skipping stones – skating in the winter – or, for more contemplative souls, sitting on the bank daydreaming: these activities and more were available to Hannibal boys. An approaching steamboat energized the whole town. Upon seeing a plume of smoke, people hurried from their homes and shops and went to the wharf to meet the arriving vessel. The steamboats fired the daydreams of the Hannibal boys, who imagined working on one or boarding another to take them wherever they wished.

Sam often skipped school to enjoy the opportunities for fun and adventure Hannibal offered. Afraid his father would whip him for missing school one day, Sam hesitated to return home that night. Instead he climbed through the open window into his father's office to sleep on the sofa. Once his eyes grew accustomed to the dark, he noticed a dead body on the office floor. The chest was exposed, and he could see a ghastly stab wound. He jumped out the window and ran home fast. He learned that the man, who had been stabbed nearby and carried into the office to be doctored, perished within an hour. Retelling the story in *Innocents Abroad* to illustrate the

Boyhood Experience, engraving, from Mark Twain, *The Innocents Abroad, or The New Pilgrims' Progress* (1870), p. 176.

difficulty of forgetting repulsive things, Twain admitted, 'I have slept in the same room with him often, since then – in my dreams.'[20]

Jane Clemens also made Sam attend Sunday school. Joshua Richmond, his Sunday school teacher, left a lasting impression – in terms of body, if not soul. A stonemason by trade, Richmond had hit his thumb with a hammer, resulting in a thumbnail that was 'permanently twisted and distorted and curved and pointed, like a parrot's beak'.[21] Mr Richmond used to award students with blue tickets for reciting Bible verses from memory. According to his autobiography, Sam memorized one set of verses and recited them every Sunday to earn enough tickets to borrow a book from the Sunday school library:

> They were pretty dreary books, for there was not a bad boy in the entire bookcase. They were *all* good boys and good girls and

drearily uninteresting, but they were better society than none, and I was glad to have their company and disapprove of it.[22]

This anecdote downplays Sam's youthful knowledge of the Bible, but personal letters from his late teens and early twenties give the lie to the anecdote: Sam knew the Holy Scriptures much better than he pretended. Biblical verses often appear in his writings. In *Innocents Abroad* he upholds the Bible as a literary model, praising its simplicity of language, felicity of expression and capacity for 'making the narrative stand out alone and seem to tell itself'.[23]

Regardless of what it shows about Clemens's knowledge of the Bible, the Sunday school anecdote reveals a boy who loved to read but was sometimes starved for reading material. Marshall Clemens had a law library but never assembled a belletristic collection. He would become a shareholder in the town library, but its modest collection could not quench Sam's thirst for reading. Jane Clemens, whose tastes ran towards self-help books and devotional literature, owned few volumes that interested her son.[24] Sam was so desperate for printed matter he read whatever he could, even insipid books about do-good boys who obeyed their parents, went to school, said their prayers and washed behind the ears.

Little is known about what other books Sam read in his youth. 'Villagers of 1840–3', a reminiscence of Hannibal and its citizenry he wrote over fifty years later, lists five authors whose works were popular during his boyhood: Lord Byron, James Fenimore Cooper, Charles Dickens, Frederick Marryat and Sir Walter Scott. Clemens did not intend this set of names as a recommended reading list. He would enjoy Dickens, but Scott and Cooper gave him fits. Sam preferred imaginary voyages, such as *Robinson Crusoe* and *Gulliver's Travels.* In his correspondence he recalls reading *Gulliver's Travels* as a boy and gloating over 'its prodigies and its marvels'.[25]

The *Arabian Nights*, another book filled with marvels and prodigies, was a special favourite. Chance encounters helped Sam remember the book time and again. Seeing a camel train in Smyrna, for instance, brought the *Arabian Nights* to mind:

> It casts you back at once into your forgotten boyhood, and again you dream over the wonders of the Arabian Nights; again your companions are princes, your lord is the Caliph Haroun Al Raschid, and your servants are terrific giants and genii that come with smoke and lightning and thunder, and go as a storm goes when they depart![26]

Few passages in his work better reveal what books meant to Sam during his boyhood. They fired his imagination, taking him to magical worlds. Their characters provided him with a nearly inexhaustible set of companions whom he could summon at will. The books themselves were companions – a figurative comparison he would often use to describe favourite literary works.

From his arrival in Hannibal with his family, Sam progressed through a series of schools. First he attended a dame school, after which he transferred to a common school for boys and girls kept by William O. Cross, 'one of the old-time teachers who believed that a good "licking" now and then helped mightily in educating a boy'. Nancy Rowland remembered her fellow student well: 'Sam was a bright boy. He always knew his lessons and he was particularly good on history and astronomy. Then he could go to the blackboard and work out the hardest example in no time.'[27]

Sam next attended a school kept by John D. Dawson. Instead of describing Dawson's school in his autobiography, he directs readers to its fictional equivalent, Mr Dobbins's school in *Tom Sawyer*. Will Bowen, one of Dawson's students, was Sam's best friend in Hannibal and the model for Joe Harper in *Tom Sawyer*. During a measles epidemic in Hannibal, Sam, as he tells the story, grew weary of waiting for death. Once Will caught the measles, Sam sneaked over to his house and crawled into bed with him. He caught the measles and almost died.[28] Will and Sam would reunite as adults once both turned to the Mississippi River for their livelihood.

Mark Twain based the character of Tom Sawyer at least partly on himself. Years later he would call his schooldays in Hannibal his 'Tom Sawyer days'. He based Huckleberry Finn on Tom Blankenship, the son of the town drunkard, who never made his boy go to school. Tom Blankenship was, in Twain's words, 'ignorant, unwashed, insufficiently fed; but he had as good a heart as ever any boy had'.[29]

Upon reading *Tom Sawyer*, Indiana newspaperwoman Henrietta Cosgrove sensed that Twain had based the title character on his boyhood self. When she asked his mother for confirmation, Jane Clemens, with a 'merry twinkle' in her eye, replied, 'He was more like Huckleberry Finn.'[30] There may have been a little Huckleberry Finn in Sam Clemens, but, then again, isn't there a little Huckleberry Finn in every boy?

Marshall Clemens died on 24 March 1847. After the funeral, his widow tried to get Sam to attend school more diligently, but he still resisted. Continuing her conversation with Henrietta Cosgrove, she explained, 'I concluded to let him go into a printing office to learn the trade, as I couldn't have him running wild.'[31] Jane Clemens's words suggest that Sam quit school when he began to work as a printer's apprentice, but he continued to attend school intermittently after entering the print shop. Sam was apprenticed to Henry La Cossitt, editor and proprietor of the Hannibal *Gazette*, in 1847, the same year he entered Dawson's school. The following year Sam became apprentice to Joseph P. Ament, who had just moved his *Missouri Courier* from Palmyra to Hannibal. Sam kept going to school at least until 1849.[32]

A newspaper printing office gave Sam something the schoolhouse did not: an almost limitless supply of reading material. Discussing the lifelong habit of cigar smoking he developed at the print shop, Twain incidentally revealed the source of all this reading material.

A shopkeeper in Hannibal who sold locally rolled cigars let him and a fellow apprentice have in trade all the cheap cigars – 'Garth's Damnedest' – they could smoke: 'We used to trade old newspapers (exchanges) for that brand.'[33] Exchanges: that solo parenthetical indicates the world of literature Sam entered when he became a printer's apprentice.

During the early-to-mid-nineteenth century, newspaper offices commonly exchanged newspapers with one another. Ament, like newspaper editors across the nation, established bilateral exchange agreements with his peers. According to one contemporary estimate, every newspaper then published in the United States received over three hundred exchanges each month.[34] Ament received so many papers that neither he nor his apprentices could read them all, so they traded their surplus for Garth's Damnedest Cigars.

These newspaper exchanges formed the backbone of the news-gathering process in antebellum America. They also helped disseminate belletristic literature. Editors took the latest news stories and feature articles from other newspapers. Tales and sketches were frequently transmitted from one paper to another. During the dozen years after Longstreet published *Georgia Scenes*, the best newspaper literature in the United States exemplified the humour of the Old Southwest. Comical stories about drinking, fighting, gambling, hunting, horse racing and horse trading, as well as tales of backwoodsmen, charlatans, colonels, dandies, greenhorns, quacks, rogues, swindlers and all sorts of oddballs and eccentrics, filled the columns of the sporting magazines, humorous weeklies and daily newspapers.

After Orion Clemens established a newspaper and job printing office in Hannibal, he hired Sam in January 1851 to work for him as a journeyman printer. Sam served as both typesetter and editorial assistant for his brother's weekly paper, the Hannibal *Journal*. Like Joseph Ament, Orion developed exchange agreements that supplied him with copy and Sam with plenty of reading material in the form of sketches in the Old Southwest tradition. These newspaper writings challenged many aspiring writers across the South.[35] In Sam Clemens's case, they fuelled his desire to become an author and gave him literary models to follow. Sam wrote occasional squibs and a brief anecdote or two for the Hannibal *Journal*, but by the time he was sixteen he longed to flex his creative muscles, to write for a paper with a national readership.

Orion received the Boston *Carpet-Bag*, a humorous weekly, as an exchange. Founded in 1851, the *Carpet-Bag* established an excellent reputation, attracting some of the nation's funniest writers during its first year.[36] Under the initials 's.l.c.' Sam submitted 'The Dandy Frightening the Squatter' to the *Carpet-Bag*, which accepted the four-hundred-word tale for publication. It appeared in the 1 May 1852 issue.

This, Sam's first published short story, proved to be a perennial favourite with the newspaper-reading public. Though its contemporary reprints have hitherto gone unnoticed, 'The Dandy Frightening the Squatter' reappeared numerous times over the next decade under different titles. Its circulation shows how the newspaper exchange system disseminated literature across the nation. In Nyack, New York, the *Rockland County Journal* reprinted the story with the original title under its author's initials two months after it had appeared in Boston. The initials soon disappeared from the reprints, and editors felt free to retitle the story and edit it to suit. Using a key phrase from its text, the *Onondaga Gazette* in Baldwinsville, New York, reprinted the story under the title 'Drilling Key Holes'.[37]

The story drifted south over the next two years. In Danville the *Kentucky Tribune* reprinted it in 1853 as 'Didn't Scare Him Bad'. The following year the tale appeared in Virginia and Tennessee. Another exchange returned it to Nyack in 1856, when the *Rockland County Journal* reprinted it again. Renewed enthusiasm for the tale prompted numerous reprints across the South. After it appeared in the *American Organ*, a Washington daily, in March 1856, it was reprinted in Maryland, North Carolina and Tennessee. Other newspapers from New York to South Carolina republished the story in the late 1850s. It remained in circulation into the next decade, being reprinted from Ohio to Kansas.[38]

'The Dandy Frightening the Squatter' fits squarely within the Old Southwest tradition. The story's title is ironic: the dandy never does frighten the squatter. Instead, the squatter turns the tables on the dandy. In the humour of the Old Southwest, outsiders – city slickers, dandies, Yankees – typically arrive on the scene with a sense of superiority only to get their comeuppance as a lesson in humility from a local inhabitant.

'Squatter' means roughly the same as 'backwoodsman'. The story itself describes the character as 'a tall, brawny woodsman' who lives among other squatters in Hannibal, Missouri. 'The Dandy and the Squatter' is the story in which Clemens contrasts Hannibal in 1852 with its earlier condition as a scarcely populated woodyard in 1839, when the story is set. With this tale Clemens first acknowledged Hannibal's potential as a literary setting and idealized its past.

The squatter stands leaning against a tree as a steamboat approaches. Aboard is a 'spruce young dandy, with a killing moustache' trying to impress the pretty female passengers. Seeing the squatter, the dandy tells the young women that he will frighten him into a conniption. Preparing himself, the dandy thrusts a Bowie knife in his belt and takes a horse-pistol in either hand. Equipped with these oversized weapons, the dandy strikes a laughable pose. Ashore he confronts the squatter. Pointing his pistols at him, the dandy exclaims, 'You'll make a capital barn door, and I shall drill the key-hole myself!' Undaunted, the squatter plants a huge fist between the dandy's eyes, sending him smack into the river. As the dandy sneaks back to the boat, the squatter accosts him, 'I say, yeou, next time yeou come around drillin' key-holes, dont forget yer old

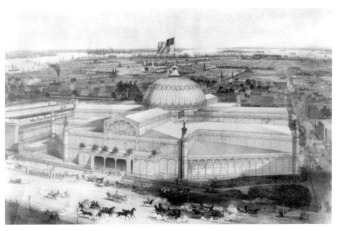

John Bachmann, *Bird's Eye View of the New York Crystal Palace and Environs*, 1853, lithograph.

acquaintances!' The young women unanimously award the knife and pistols to the squatter.[39]

'The Dandy Frightening the Squatter' may not be great literature, but it is great fun. If nothing else, it shows where Clemens began as a writer, providing a benchmark to indicate how he would progress. The dialect spellings – 'yeou' and 'yer' – demonstrate an early attempt to capture the way people talk, something Clemens would perfect by the time he reached *Huckleberry Finn*.[40] Clemens has the dandy 'floundering in the turbid waters of the Mississippi'. When he would write 'Old Times on the Mississippi' two decades later, such vague, nondescript characterizations would yield to lyrical phrases like 'the majestic, the magnificent Mississippi, rolling its mile-wide tide along, shining in the sun'.[41]

Sam continued working for Orion into June 1853, when, in his own words, he 'disappeared one night and fled to St. Louis'.[42] He moved in with their sister Pamela, who had married a St Louis businessman named William A. Moffett. Sam found work as a typesetter for the *Evening News*. Two months later he abruptly left town. Via steamboat and railway he travelled to Monroe, Michigan, where he caught the *Southern Michigan*, a steamer Clemens called a 'fine Lake palace', demonstrating his pleasure in luxury transportation. The memorably choppy crossing of Lake Erie left him happy to be on land again. Once the *Southern Michigan* docked at Buffalo, he took the railway to Albany and the steamer *Isaac Newton* down the Hudson to New York.[43]

The World's Fair gave Clemens the excuse to visit New York. Like thousands of other tourists, he marvelled over the Crystal Palace, but, unlike most of them, he lingered in the city to find work. John A. Gray, the proprietor of a vast printing plant responsible for producing the day's best magazines, hired him to set type. Since Gray did not pay very well, Clemens had little spending money. Happily, the Printers' Free Library and Reading Room at 3 Chambers Street was only a few blocks from his boarding house. Sam wrote to his mother, reassuring her that he spent his evenings at the library: 'If books are not good company, where will I find it?'[44]

In the third week of October Clemens left New York for Philadelphia, becoming a substitute typesetter for the *Inquirer*.

A. Janicke & Co., *Our City (St. Louis, Mo.)*, 1859, lithograph.

In his brother's absence Orion Clemens had sold the Hannibal *Journal* and relocated to Muscatine, Iowa. 'How do you like "free-soil"?' Sam asked his brother, acknowledging that Orion had relocated from Missouri, a slave state, to Iowa, a free state.[45] Orion liked it just fine. His residency in Iowa would create opportunities unavailable in Missouri after the Civil War broke out.

Orion encouraged Sam to contribute letters from Philadelphia to the Muscatine *Journal*, the newspaper he had recently founded. Sam complied. Cribbed from local news articles, his letters to the *Journal* lack the charm of his family correspondence. Sam could write better when he ignored source material and cultivated his personal voice. On a flying visit from Philadelphia to Washington, for example, he described how disorganized the residences in the U.S. capital seemed: 'They look as though they might have been emptied out of a sack by some Brobdignagian gentleman, and when falling, been scattered abroad by the winds.'[46] While reflecting Sam's knowledge of *Gulliver's Travels,* this sentence reveals his ability to create vivid and original imagery.

In his literary development Clemens's time in Philadelphia involved stockpiling images and ideas for future use. Peopled by memorable characters, the boarding house where he lived was ripe for literary treatment. Years later he acknowledged how powerful a boarding-house setting could be after reading Balzac's *Père Goriot*.[47] His Philadelphia boarding house would provide the setting for a humorous sketch he titled 'Jul'us Caesar'. As the story goes, Clemens and a friend convince a fellow boarder to try his hand at poetry. This would-be poet, a thick-headed dolt whose classical nickname stems from his favourite oath, takes their suggestion and starts versifying with hilarious consequences.[48]

Despite how much he enjoyed Philadelphia, Clemens had trouble making ends meet. In early 1854 he joined his brothers and mother in Muscatine but relocated to St Louis that summer, re-joining Pamela's family. By late May 1856 he had moved to Keokuk, Iowa, where Orion, having married a local girl, established the Ben Franklin Book and Job Office. Sam helped his brother print the city directory. Listing his own name and occupation, Sam identified himself as an 'antiquarian'. His passion for history may have had something to do with the profession he claimed, but a local story that circulated orally traces Sam's antiquarian interests to 'his researches among the ancient and venerable bugs of the hotel in which he boarded'.[49]

Restless and suggestible – a dangerous combination – Clemens read William Lewis Herndon's *Exploration of the Valley of the Amazon,* which gave him the idea to visit Brazil and export indigenous plant material with miraculous powers: coca (not cocoa, as child-friendly biographies assert). Clemens's dream of becoming a Brazilian drug lord is the first of many harebrained money-making schemes that would capture his attention and fuel his unshakeable desire for fabulous wealth. Longing to ascend the Amazon and 'open up a trade in coca with all the world', as he would explain in 'The Turning Point of My Life', the fine autobiographical essay he would write near the end of life, Sam left Keokuk in October 1856 but ended up in Ohio, not Brazil.[50] In Cincinnati he found work with a leading printer.

Reviving his Brazilian dreams, Clemens left Cincinnati in April 1857 aboard the *Paul Jones* on its way South. On the river he pondered a new career, deciding to become a Mississippi river boat pilot. His mother, who always worried about the company he kept, was disappointed to learn Sam's latest career plans. She told Henrietta Cosgrove, 'I gave him up then, for I always thought steamboating was a wicked business, and was sure he would meet bad associates.'[51]

A refuge for gamblers and prostitutes and confidence tricksters, the steamboat did contain many bad elements, but Jane Clemens overstated their wickedness. As Thomas Bangs Thorpe suggests in 'The Big Bear of Arkansas' – the pinnacle of Old Southwestern humour – the Mississippi riverboat was a microcosm. Thorpe set his story on a steamboat peopled by numerous character types: an aristocratic Southern plantation owner, an English sportsman, a Yankee peddler and representative men from states newly carved from the Old Northwest: Buckeyes, Hoosiers, Suckers and Wolverines. Clemens was astonished by all the characters he encountered during his days as a riverboat pilot. In *Life on the Mississippi* he says that whenever he found a well-drawn character in a novel or a biography, he would 'take a warm personal interest in him, for the reason that I have known him before – met him on the river'.[52]

Aboard the *Paul Jones* Clemens met Horace Bixby, a gruff but lovable man and an excellent river pilot. Clemens convinced Bixby to train him. As his cub, Clemens began learning the river, an arduous task he would describe in *Life on the Mississippi*. Though highly crafted and partly fictionalized, the book captures the joy and frustration Clemens experienced as he became a pilot, from his heart-breaking realization that he had to learn the Mississippi in not just one but *both* directions to the awareness that he had to know its concave shores well enough to negotiate the river in the dark. As Bixby told him, he needed to understand it 'with such absolute

A Steamboat Race on the Mississippi (between the Baltic and Diana), 1859, lithograph.

certainty that you can always steer by the shape that's *in your head*, and never mind the one that's before your eyes'.[53]

To read a person's face like a book was a proverbial comparison long before Twain's time. He breathed new life into this traditional simile while describing how he came to know the river:

> The face of the water, in time, became a wonderful book – a book that was a dead language to the uneducated passenger, but which told its mind to me without reserve, delivering its most cherished secrets as clearly as if it uttered them with a voice. And it was not a book to be read once and thrown aside, for it had a new story to tell every day. Throughout the long twelve hundred miles there was never a page that was void of interest, never one that you could leave unread without loss, never one that you would want to skip, thinking you could find higher enjoyment in some other thing. There never was so wonderful a book written by man; never one whose interest was so absorbing, so unflagging, so sparklingly renewed with every re-perusal.[54]

In the coming years Clemens would reverse the simile: he would read books as he used to read the river. To careful readers, books deliver secrets that untrained readers never understand. Every reading yields new ideas and provokes further thought.

As a cub, Clemens also served under William Brown, a pilot on the *Pennsylvania*. In addition Sam secured a place on the boat for his younger brother Henry as third or 'mud' clerk. After an altercation in New Orleans, Brown left Sam ashore when the *Pennsylvania* returned upriver the second week of June 1858. Later that week the boat exploded, killing over a hundred people. Coming upriver on another boat, Sam found Henry mortally wounded in Memphis, where the survivors had been taken. After Henry's death Sam came down with survivor's guilt, a chronic affliction in his case.[55]

The tragedy did not stop Sam, who was only 22, from pursuing his career as a pilot. By August he was back on the river. A man who frequently travelled up and down the Mississippi met Sam around this time and described him as 'a gaunt young fellow, with sleepy Southern manners and a drawl peculiar to the river town in Missouri'.[56] Sam continued to work hard and, on 9 April 1859, earned his pilot's licence. He took pride in his knowledge but sadly realized it had taken a toll: 'I had lost something which could never be restored to me while I lived. All the grace, the beauty, the poetry had gone out of the majestic river!'[57]

Learning the river left Clemens little time to write, but after becoming a pilot he put his professional knowledge to creative use. In early 1861 he wrote 'Ghost Life on the Mississippi', the finest short story to emerge from his pilot years. The narrator retells a supernatural tale he had heard from a respected river pilot named Joseph Millard, whose personal story must be prefaced with that of William Jones, the 'king of pilots' who had met a tragic end while running the 'Graveyard', that is, the treacherous channel along Goose Island. Navigating the same passage on a snowy night, Millard felt another presence in the pilot house before seeing a monstrous apparition:

> In an instant the wheel was jerked out of his hands,
> and a sudden gleam of light from a crack in the stove
> pipe revealed the ghastly features of William Jones, with
> a great piece of skin, ragged and bloody, torn loose from
> his forehead and dangling and flapping over his left eye –
> the other eye dead and fixed and lustreless – hair wet and
> disordered, and the whole body bent and shapeless, like
> that of a drowned man, and apparently rigid as marble,
> except the hands and arms, which seemed alone endued
> with life and motion![58]

Like 'The Golden Arm', 'Ghost Life on the Mississippi' reflects Twain's interest in the supernatural, which may seem at odds with the literary realism he has come to represent. It is not. Clemens's interest in folktales and legends suits his fascination with the vernacular, his effort to explore what people believe and how they talk. Regardless of its subject matter, this passage illustrates Clemens's growing narrative powers. His conjoined descriptors deliberately pace his narrative and enhance its creepiness.

Clemens never published 'Ghost Life on the Mississippi'. With the Civil War, every aspect of American life was a shambles. After spending a few days with Pamela and her family in St Louis in late April 1861, Sam left for New Orleans the first week of May. He apparently returned to St Louis aboard the *Nebraska*, the last boat to gain free passage to the upper Mississippi through the Union blockade at Memphis. Reaching St Louis on 21 May 1861, he had also reached the end of his career as a river pilot, which he had intended to pursue into the foreseeable future. Even after establishing himself as a popular author, Clemens still lamented the loss of his career as a river pilot: 'I loved the profession far better than any I have followed since, and I took a measureless pride in it.'[59]

Once he began writing professionally, Clemens found a lasting way to commemorate his lost career: he would borrow his pen name from an exclamation commonly heard aboard a Mississippi steamboat. Pilots often had their leadsmen take soundings to measure the river's depth. To designate when the ship reached a safe depth – two fathoms – a leadsman would shout, 'Mark twain!' The name that Clemens took as a writer signals his former profession as a riverboat pilot.

Three months before his piloting career came to an abrupt and unexpected end, Clemens found himself in New Orleans with time on his hands, so he went to Custom House Street to see the one and only Madame Caprell, the 'great and wonderful clairvoyant', to

Portrait of Samuel Clemens as a youth holding a printer's composing stick with the letters S A M.

quote her own publicity. Millicent Holliday, who often travelled the river, had urged Sam to visit Madame Caprell for a psychic reading. On a lark he took her suggestion. Sam related the episode in a letter to Orion written months before he knew his career as a pilot was doomed.[60] According to the letter, this Crescent City soothsayer told him: 'You have written a great deal; you write well – but you are rather out of practice; no matter – you will be *in* practice some day.'

2

Doings in Nevada

When Sam Clemens returned to Hannibal in June 1861 he and some friends from town banded together to form the Marion Rangers, a volunteer Confederate regiment. They were motivated more by a sense of fun than a will to fight. Since all of them were townies, they had little experience of camping, riding or shooting. Their ensuing military activities mainly involved wriggling through the mud, brush and brambles while retreating from whatever Union troops were rumoured to be around. The Marion Rangers did enjoy some special moments. Occasionally a farmer would treat them to a Missouri country breakfast: bacon and eggs, biscuits, corn pone, fried chicken and coffee. Evenings they spent around the campfire singing songs and spinning yarns. But the hardships outweighed the good times. After a couple of weeks, Clemens had had enough of soldiering and quietly returned to St Louis. Despite its brevity, the experience left a lasting impression, which he would retell with well-seasoned hyperbole as 'A Private History of a Campaign that Failed'.[1]

Sam reached St Louis to find Orion planning to travel west. A friend in Abraham Lincoln's cabinet had helped Orion secure an appointment as secretary of Nevada Territory. He asked Sam to accompany him as his personal secretary. Sam accepted, effectively disengaging himself from any further military service during the Civil War. Starting a journey that would take nearly a month, the Clemens brothers steamed up the Missouri to St Joseph and then travelled in a mail coach to Carson City, a 1,700-mile trek that would inspire the first twenty chapters of *Roughing It*, in which Mark Twain recalls the 'gladness and the wild sense of freedom that used to make the blood dance in my veins on those fine overland mornings!'[2]

At Salt Lake City, according to *Roughing It*, the Clemens brothers stocked up on provisions, obtaining a sufficient quantity of bread, ham and hard-boiled eggs to last the final 600 miles. They broke up that distance to stop and enjoy the scenery. In a beautifully cadenced passage that uses repetition while gradually amassing new details, Twain captures these simple pleasures:

> And it was comfort in those succeeding days to sit up and contemplate the majestic panorama of mountains and valleys spread out below us and eat ham and hard boiled eggs while our spiritual natures reveled alternately in rainbows, thunderstorms, and peerless sunsets. Nothing helps scenery like ham and eggs. Ham and eggs, and after these a pipe – an old, rank, delicious pipe – ham and eggs and scenery, a 'down grade,' a flying coach, a fragrant pipe and a contented heart – these make happiness. It is what all the ages have struggled for.[3]

The version of their transcontinental journey Twain tells in *Roughing It* shows how he transformed personal experience into literature through the process of elaboration. The running gag about the unabridged dictionary they supposedly brought with them offers another good example. As they try to sleep atop mail sacks inside the coach, the dictionary ricochets back and forth, hitting one man or the other on every pass. Besides providing slapstick humour, the dictionary symbolizes the brothers' ignorance of the West. Naively assuming they were headed into uncivilized territory, they brought the dictionary along to help them preserve their language, and hence their culture, from deterioration.

As the humour builds, it reveals how absurd the concept of an unabridged dictionary is. Presumably containing all the words in the language, it possesses a finality, a sense of completion, but, as Twain well knew, the English language is ever changing, ever evolving and expanding. The Far West gave rise to many new words that intrigued Sam and that he would put to literary use. The arrival of the Clemens brothers in Nevada almost instantly rendered the dictionary obsolete. Recording the changes the language underwent during the settling of the American West, *Roughing It* implicitly challenges the authority of the unabridged dictionary.

When Sam and Orion reached Carson City on 14 August 1861, six weeks remained before the territorial legislature would convene, so Sam went exploring. In mid-September he and John D. Kinney, a young Cincinnati banker, visited Lake Tahoe. Encircled by snow-capped peaks, Lake Tahoe stunned them with its majesty. The lake's beauty did not blunt their entrepreneurial impulses. Clemens and Kinney decided to enter the timber trade and staked a claim nearby. To protect their claim, they built a rudimentary fence and a lean-to, but Clemens accidentally set their camp on fire. With the ground carpeted in pine needles, the fire spread rapidly. Clemens was at the lake shore retrieving supplies when he saw the flames; Kinney was trapped on the other side and had to pass through fire to reach Clemens. They climbed into their boat, saving themselves by rowing into the lake, where they could watch the woods burn from the safety of the water until the fire extinguished itself and the night went dark.[4]

During the first session of the territorial legislature, which ran from 1 October to 29 November 1861, Sam clerked for Orion. The experience acquainted them with many local politicians, including William H. Barstow, whose friendship would prove useful once Sam became a professional journalist. Sam hesitated to turn journalist too soon, hoping to strike it rich prospecting for silver. Since he and

Orion reached Nevada shortly after the discovery of the vast silver deposit known as the Comstock Lode, Sam turned prospector upon completing his clerkship and collecting his salary.

In December 1861 he left Carson City for the Humboldt mining region with three other men. In addition to provisions and supplies – 'bacon, flour, beans, blasting-powder, picks and shovels' – they tucked a few luxury items into the spare nooks and crannies of their wagon bed: a cribbage board, fourteen decks of cards, a small keg of lager beer and a copy of Charles Dickens's *Dombey and Son*.[5]

The bacon spiced up their other provisions – 'Bacon would improve the flavor of an angel!' Sam exclaimed – but the Dickens novel proved to be the most precious item in their wagon. Sam came to know the book so well he could recall passages from memory. Allusions to *Dombey and Son* and *Martin Chuzzlewit* are among the few literary references in his early personal letters from Nevada. He especially liked Captain Cuttle in *Dombey and Son.* With a hook for a hand and a mouth full of saws and sayings, Captain Cuttle, in Clemens's view, was as humorous a character as any in literature.[6]

After the Humboldt trip, Clemens went to the Esmeralda mining district on the disputed boundary between Nevada and California. His letters from Esmeralda show how obsessed he had become. Silver seems his sole concern: where to find it, how to stake a claim and establish a mining company, when to buy and sell stock ('feet') in other silver mining companies and whether to invest in wildcat claims. He longed to become a silver baron: another version of his dream of quick and easy wealth. Years later he would make greed the villain of 'The Villagers of 1840–3'. The California Gold Rush, he says, 'begot the lust for money which is the rule of life to-day, and the hardness and cynicism which is the spirit of to-day'.[7] What he does not admit in 'Villagers' is that he, too, was struck by the greed and concomitant cynicism precious metals can induce. Though he never succeeded as a silver miner, he would continue to pursue investments that promised incredible wealth.

T. L. Dawes, *Mining on the Comstock*, 1877, lithograph.

Clemens's literary desire resurfaced in mid-1862, when he contributed some letters to the Virginia City *Territorial Enterprise*. The previous year Joseph T. Goodman, a typesetter for the San Francisco *Golden Era* – one of the earliest literary journals in the American West – had relocated to Virginia City, where he became chief editor and part owner of the *Enterprise*. Joe Goodman – whose surname sounds like the type name of a hero on the Restoration stage – turned the small and struggling weekly into the main daily newspaper on the Comstock Lode. Under his leadership the *Enterprise* published the most complete and reliable coverage of mining activity in Nevada. He turned the *Enterprise* into 'one of the cleverest and most widely read journals on the Pacific Coast'.[8]

Goodman succeeded partly because he surrounded himself with top-quality employees at every level and gave them the freedom to do their jobs. Steve Gillis, for one, was the foreman of the printing room, but, being a kind-hearted, helpful soul, he assisted the editorial

Charles Conrad Kuchel, after a drawing by Grafton T. Brown, *Virginia City, Nevada Territory*, 1861, lithograph.

department when necessary.[9] Gillis and Clemens became close friends at the *Enterprise*. Barstow worked in the newspaper's business office but also supplied editorial advice. He helped Clemens publish a series of letters to the *Enterprise* signed 'Josh'.

Dan De Quille, local editor of the *Enterprise*, was born William Wright near Frederickstown, Ohio, in 1829. He later moved to Iowa, where he married and started a family. Wright left his wife and children for California in the 1850s. With the discovery of silver he came to Nevada. After failing as a prospector, he joined the *Enterprise*. Once he chose 'Dan De Quille' as his pen name, it virtually supplanted his personal identity.[10]

Fire has taken a heavy toll on the *Enterprise* archives. Many articles De Quille wrote do not survive. Clemens's contributions to the paper have suffered a similar fate. His Josh letters have disappeared, but a reference in his family correspondence situates them within his career. While the series was running in the *Enterprise*, Sam told Orion, 'Put all of Josh's letters in my scrap book. I may have use for them some day.'[11] The correspondence says nothing more about how he might use them, but he apparently saw the collected letters as the basis for a book. Clemens would contribute hundreds of items to the newspapers and periodical press over the next few years, but he envisioned a literary career beyond journalism, foreseeing himself as a best-selling author.

On the strength of Josh's letters and Barstow's recommendation, Goodman offered Clemens the local editorship of the *Enterprise* to replace De Quille, who was planning an extended visit to his family in Iowa. Aware of Sam's experience clerking in the legislature, Goodman assumed he would be a good political reporter and, as the brother of Secretary Clemens, knew he could be an important political influence.[12]

Leaving Esmeralda and his faded dreams of becoming a silver baron, Sam Clemens entered the *Enterprise* office with a lean and hungry look. He began working for the paper in late September 1862. That same year Rollin M. Daggett joined the *Enterprise* as a reporter. Having learned the printing trade in Defiance, Ohio, Daggett came to California in 1850 to find gold. After some modest success during his first two years, he quit mining and returned to the printing trade, this time as co-owner and founding editor of the *Golden Era*. Daggett had a fierce, uncompromising literary style Clemens found appealing.[13] With Goodman, De Quille and Daggett on the staff, Clemens had much guidance as he started writing for the *Enterprise*.

Clemens hardly needed any literary guides, as 'Petrified Man', his earliest known contribution to the *Enterprise* after joining its staff, reveals. Though barely three hundred words long, 'Petrified Man' was a sensation. Written to spoof similar newspaper reports of ossified or fossilized creatures, 'Petrified Man', like all the best hoaxes, was taken seriously by many readers. Newspapers around the globe reported the story, usually abridged and partly paraphrased. In Ohio the *Fremont Journal* repeated the story but omitted the best part: Clemens's description of the petrified man's hands.[14]

Into this brief story of a Nevada man who had turned to stone Clemens built sufficient detail to reveal his humorous intent and let keen readers recognize the hoax. Describing the petrified man's appearance, he reports how the man had been holding his hands at the moment he turned to stone. His right thumb touches his nose with 'the fingers of the right hand spread apart'.[15] Clemens has been lauded for his use of folk speech in his writings; his use of folk gesture is no less impressive. In this sketch he depicts a man who was petrified while making the Shanghai gesture. With 'Petrified Man' Clemens thumbs his nose at the newspaper's readers: a bold statement for a budding journalist to make.

In November Clemens went to Carson City to cover the second session of the territorial legislature. He divided his time between reporting legislative activities and writing fanciful articles that let his wit sparkle. Developing his style, he turned a real-life friend into a stooge to serve as his comedic foil. In Clemens's reports from Carson City, fellow reporter Clement T. Rice became the 'Unreliable', an amusing character with an insatiable appetite for food and drink but no social graces.

Clemens also reported other Carson City events. In 'The Pah-Utes' he describes a new fraternal organization limited to Nevada pioneers who had arrived before the mining rush of May 1860. Clemens celebrates 'these knotty and rugged old pioneers – who have beheld Nevada in her infancy', appreciating how they prospected with no idea whether they would find any precious metals. They camped under sagebrush with lizards, horny toads and tarantulas; they smoked from the same pipe, ate from the same pot and chugged white lightning from the same flask. He paints what Joe Coulombe calls 'a happy portrait of male freedom, adventure, and camaraderie'. Clemens's portrayal of the Nevada pioneers has a tone of nostalgia, a mood that would affect his best writings. By banding together now, he continued, these 'weather-beaten and blasted old patriarchs' will be able to 'rehearse the deeds of the hoary past, and rescue its traditions from oblivion!'[16]

Once the legislature adjourned in December, Clemens went back to Virginia City, arriving in time to say goodbye to De Quille. He reported Dan's farewell as a mock elegy, 'The Illustrious Departed'. Though this article represents Clemens's first contribution to the local column in De Quille's absence, it shows how well he understood its typical contents. A dearth of local news, he asserts, led to Dan's demise:

> He fell under a scarcity of pack-trains and hay-wagons. These had been the bulwark of the local column; his confidence in them was like unto that which men have in four aces; murders, robberies, fires, distinguished arrivals, were creatures of chance, which might or might not occur at any moment; but the pack-trains and the hay-wagons were certain, predestined, immutable! When these failed last week, he said '*Et tu Brute*', and gave us his pen.[17]

Closing the essay, Clemens hoped De Quille's trip across the Plains would restore him to 'his ancient health and energy'.[18]

Though brief, 'The Illustrious Departed' shows Clemens doing something he would do in his greatest works, that is, taking realistic material and imbuing it with mythic qualities. Clemens knew from first-hand experience the hardships of crossing the continent in the days before the transcontinental railroad, but he does not mention them, trading reality for symbolism. Stressing the restorative power of the American Plains, he celebrates the land's natural fecundity: rich and fertile, it can bring the dead to life. In Clemens's hands, a stagecoach trip across the Trans-Mississippi West is akin to a mythical journey that transforms the traveller into a new person.

Upon hiring Clemens, Goodman got the impression that 'in funny matters he was much oftener the jokee than the joker'.

Goodman theorized that his humour developed as a defence mechanism. Clemens quickly endeared himself to those around him. He could turn on the charm as well as he could turn a phrase. William M. Stewart, a local attorney who specialized in untangling the tangled litigation that mining claims created, called him 'the most lovable scamp and nuisance who ever blighted Nevada'.[19]

After barely a month at the *Enterprise* Clemens convinced Goodman to give him a week's holiday. He left for Carson City in late January, promising to send reports back to the newspaper. Stewart remembered Clemens writing 'ridiculous pieces about parties and other social events'.[20] 'Letter from Carson City' describes one such party hosted by the governor. This letter, which appeared in the 3 February 1863 issue of the *Enterprise*, Clemens wrote as 'Mark Twain'.

'Letter from Carson City' represents his earliest known use of the pen name. Since the files of the *Enterprise* have been so thoroughly destroyed, other, possibly earlier, Twain letters do not survive, but something Sam told his mother shows him carefully crafting this new persona. He explained how he emphasized Mark Twain's origins: 'I never let an opportunity slip to blow my horn for Missouri.' Far more than a pen name, Mark Twain would become Clemens's public identity. As in De Quille's case, the pseudonym practically usurped the author's identity. He even tried signing a letter to his mother 'Mark', but she quashed that idea.[21] In public he could be Mark Twain, but in private he would stay Sam Clemens. For the rest of this biography he will be called Mark Twain. The literary present tense will be used to distinguish the fictional persona from the historical personage.

Weaving through a crowd of party guests in 'Letter from Carson City', Twain soon reaches the punch bowl. Who should he find there but the 'omnipresent Unreliable'. The reappearance of the Unreliable supplies some continuity with the pre-Twain contributions to the *Enterprise*. The two friendly rivals reach a mutual decision to guard the governor's punch, which rapidly disappears on their watch. Continuing to develop his new persona, Twain would send the *Enterprise* two more letters from Carson City that week.

In 'Reportorial', Twain offers a mock obituary of the Unreliable, who suddenly revives during the funeral sermon:

> The shrouded corpse shoved the coffin lid to one side, rose to a sitting posture, cocked his eye at the minister and smilingly said, 'Oh let up, Dominie, this is played out, you know – loan me two bits!' The frightened congregation rushed from the house, and the Unreliable followed them, with his coffin on his shoulder. He sold it for two dollars and a half, and got drunk at a 'bit house' on the proceeds. He is still drunk.[22]

This mock obituary for the Unreliable and the mock elegy for De Quille both represent variations on a favourite theme. The Unreliable's funeral anticipates an iconic moment in *Tom Sawyer* when Tom and Huck and Joe Harper return to St Petersburg and hide in the church gallery to listen to their own funeral sermon.

'Mark Twain' was a sensation. Readers became curious to learn about the man behind the mask and eager to read more from him. 'Reportorial', for instance, was reprinted in Western newspapers as far away as Portland, Oregon.[23] Goodman recognized a good thing when he saw it. He loosened his reins and gave him a raise. These early Twain letters taught their author an important truth: good writing can create great freedom. By May, Goodman let Twain temporarily step down as local editor to spend two months in San Francisco, provided he send letters back to the *Enterprise.* Clement Rice – the Unreliable himself – accompanied him.

'Letter from Mark Twain', published the third week of May, is the first known work to use 'Mark Twain' in its title: further evidence of its author's growing reputation in Nevada. The Unreliable enters just as he is finishing the letter. Seeing Twain cudgel his brain for something poetical to say about San Francisco weather, the Unreliable exclaims, 'Say it's bully, you tallow-brained idiot! that's enough; anybody can understand that; don't write any of those infernal, sick platitudes about sweet flowers, and joyous butterflies, and worms and things, for people to read before breakfast.'[24] The Unreliable's admonition represents an internal conflict Twain faced as he developed his literary style: the clash between safely following current standards of taste or boldly developing his own unique voice.

Twain's reputation had preceded him to San Francisco, where he received an offer to contribute letters from Nevada to the *Morning Call*. He accepted. He also agreed to contribute several humorous sketches to the *Golden Era*, which was still going strong even after Daggett had sold his interest in it. Once Twain returned to Nevada to resume the local editorship for the *Enterprise*, he continued sending letters to the *Call*.

'Unfortunate Blunder', his finest contribution to the *Call* that summer, is an anecdote playing upon the multipurpose function of public buildings in the West. On weeknights the Union League – one of several private clubs founded across the North to support the war effort – held meetings in the Virginia City Courthouse. The First Presbyterian Church held services there on Sunday mornings. As Twain tells the story, a drunken Irish member of the Union League enters the courthouse during Sunday services and, thinking he has entered a League meeting, spits and hiccoughs and begins to air his grievances, his brogue slurred by liquor and expletives. Playful sketches like this one helped spread Twain's reputation beyond San Francisco. In Santa Rosa, California, for example, the editor of the *Sonoma County Democrat* reprinted 'Unfortunate Blunder', calling it a 'rich joke'.[25]

De Quille's return from Iowa in early September 1863 freed Twain from his local responsibilities in Virginia City and let him get back to San Francisco. In the third week of September Twain published 'Curing a Cold' in the *Golden Era*. This sketch, which describes many dubious cold remedies, begins: 'It is a good thing, perhaps to write for the amusement of the public, but it is a far higher and nobler thing to write for their instruction – their profit – their actual and tangible benefit.'[26] Echoing Sydney Carton's final thoughts in *A Tale of Two Cities* ('It is a far, far better thing that I do . . .'), Twain deflates such grandiose sentiments of self-sacrifice by applying them to the decision to instruct his readers instead of delighting them. Twain speaks ironically, of course. 'Curing a Cold' offers little instruction but much delight. The sketch captured the attention of readers as far away as Oxford – Oxford, Indiana, that is. The paper there reprinted 'Curing a Cold' with the following introduction: 'Mr Mark Twain gives his experience in curing his cold in so quaint and unique a style, that we copy it in full for the benefit of our readers.'[27]

When Twain returned to Virginia City in late October, he and De Quille rented an apartment at 25 North B Street, a large brick building that also housed the Virginia City Library and Reading

Isador Laurent Deroy, *Vue de San-Francisco Vista de San-Francisco*, *c*. 1860, lithograph.

Rooms. Reading became a nightly activity for both men. Their apartment combined a large bedroom with a smaller room they used as a parlour. Together they shared a huge double bed. They made good roommates. De Quille remembered that they 'both wanted to read and smoke about the same length of time after getting into bed, and if one got hungry and got up to go down town for oysters the other also became hungry and turned out'.[28]

Like Twain and De Quille, many other American humorists used pseudonyms that practically usurped their personal identities. In Ohio, David Ross Locke created the persona of Petroleum V. Nasby, a narrow-minded preacher whose defence of ignorance and bigotry is so warped that it effectively critiques what it purports to defend. Charles Farrar Browne, then the nation's most renowned humorist, had established his reputation in Ohio as local editor of the Toledo *Commercial*. The Cleveland *Plain Dealer* snatched him from Toledo. As local editor at the *Plain Dealer*, he invented the persona of a barely literate travelling showman named Artemus Ward. Like Nasby, he peppered his work with misspellings and grammatical errors. In 1861 Artemus Ward, as Browne became known, left Ohio for New York to become managing editor of *Vanity Fair*.

Ward also found great success as a public speaker. He carried over the screwy pronunciations from his writing to his speaking. Twain savoured a joke that circulated about Ralph Waldo Emerson lecturing in such an incoherent manner that people thought he was Artemus Ward. But Ward deserves recognition for his approach to public speaking, which differed greatly from the approach to lyceum lecturing Emerson symbolized. Ward's joke-filled lectures were like nothing his audiences had ever seen or heard: Artemus Ward is the first stand-up comic in history.[29]

When Ward came to Virginia City the third week of December 1863, he made the *Enterprise* office his local headquarters. He became good friends and drinking buddies with De Quille and Twain. Ward recognized Twain's talent and urged him to 'leave sage-brush obscurity, and journey to New York with him'. Twain turned him down. As he explained to his mother, 'I preferred not to burst upon the New York public too suddenly and brilliantly, and so I concluded to remain here.'[30]

His words sound facetious, but they demonstrate how shrewd Twain had become in managing his nascent literary career. He had no intention of going to New York on the spur of the moment or on the coat-tails of Artemus Ward. Instead, he planned to burst onto the New York scene all by his lonesome. Ward also suggested he contribute to the New York *Sunday Mercury*, promising to write a letter of recommendation to its editor. Twain did not wait for Ward's recommendation. He submitted 'Doings in Nevada' to the *Mercury* on his own hook. The editor accepted the article, which appeared on the first Sunday in February 1864.

In 'Doings in Nevada' Mark Twain reports local efforts to attain statehood. He describes the proposed state seal, which was filled with icons of progress and prosperity above a Latin motto, '*Volens et Potens*' (Willing and Able). Twain has an alternate idea:

We have an animal here whose surname is the 'jackass rabbit'. It is three feet long, has legs like a counting-house stool, ears of monstrous length, and no tail to speak of. It is swifter than a greyhound, and as meek and harmless as an infant . . . Well, somebody proposed as a substitute for that pictorial Great Seal, a figure of a jackass rabbit reposing in the shade of his native sage-brush, with the motto '*Volens* enough, but not so d—d *Potens*.'[31]

The icon of a jackass rabbit reposing in the shade of the sagebrush could symbolize Twain himself in his 'sage-brush obscurity', which he was becoming anxious to escape. His increasingly controversial articles in the *Enterprise* during the spring of 1864 upset many local citizens and further motivated

Occidental Hotel, Montgomery Street, from the Russ House, San Francisco, 1866, photographic print.

his departure. On 29 May he left Virginia City with Steve Gillis on the San Francisco stagecoach. Joe Goodman came along for the ride. Goodman, who intended to travel only a few miles, enjoyed their company so much he stuck with Twain and Gillis all the way to San Francisco. Years later Goodman would recall the city in Twain's time, evoking 'the tender grace of the San Francisco he knew'. They initially settled at the Occidental Hotel or, as Twain called it, 'Heaven on the half shell'.[32]

In June Twain took a job as local reporter for the *Morning Call*. The daily work was tedious, but the *Californian*, a literary weekly owned and edited by Charles Henry Webb that featured Bret Harte as principal contributor, gave him a more creative outlet. Twain befriended both Harte and Webb, who welcomed him to submit articles, agreeing to pay $12 for each. Besides the extra income, the *Californian* would enhance Twain's nationwide reputation. He told Orion, 'The paper has an exalted reputation in the east, and is liberally copied from by papers like the *Home Journal*.'[33] After four months at the *Morning Call*, Twain could no longer tolerate the tedium of straight reporting. He quit the *Call* to follow his calling.

Living on his contributions to the *Californian*, Twain developed narrative techniques that would come to define his style. He often prefaces one subject with another, getting so carried away with the first that he never gets around to the second. His most famous instance of this technique occurs in *Roughing It* with the story of Jim Blaine and his grandfather's old ram. Blaine heaps one digression atop another but never reaches the ram. In 'A Touching Story of George Washington's Boyhood', a sketch that appeared in the *Californian* in the last week of October 1864, Twain never does get to George Washington and the cherry tree but instead spends his entire column discussing amateur musical performance.

'The Killing of Julius Caesar "Localized"', the finest article Twain wrote for the *Californian*, is an outrageous send-up of sensational news stories. By 'localized' he means converted to the manner of the local reporter, who would relate stories of murder and mayhem to suit the sensation-hungry public. Twain took the story of Caesar's assassination from the third act of Shakespeare's *Julius Caesar* and rewrote it as a local news story. It begins in the voice of a modern-day reporter who imagines 'skirmishing around old Rome, button-holing soldiers, senators and citizens by turns, and transferring "all the particulars" from them to my note-book'.[34] After his introduction, the author gives way to what is purportedly a newspaper article from Caesar's time translated from the original Latin.

Twain satirized other forms of popular discourse in his contributions to the *Californian*. In his headnote to 'Lucretia Smith's Soldier', published in the first week of December 1864, he identifies his tale with 'those nice, sickly war stories in *Harper's Weekly*'.[35] Throughout the Civil War, *Harper's Weekly* had been publishing syrupy stories set against the background of the war. Other contemporary periodicals serialized sentimental novels. 'Lucretia Smith's Soldier' spoofs both topical war fiction and the sentimental novel.

Written as a condensed novel, a genre of burlesque fiction William Makepeace Thackeray made fashionable, 'Lucretia Smith's Soldier' relates the story of Reginald de Whittaker, who visits his sweetheart Lucretia Borgia Smith to tell her he has enlisted in the Union army. Before he can speak his piece, she criticizes him for not enlisting. Incensed, he leaves her for the front. When she reads that R. D. Whittaker has been badly wounded, she visits the hospital. Finding his face covered in bandages, she devotes weeks nursing him back to health. When the bandages come off, she is shocked to discover that the soldier she has been nursing is not her erstwhile sweetheart at all but a similarly named Wisconsin soldier. She exclaims, 'O confound my cats if I haven't gone and fooled away three mortal weeks here, snuffling and slobbering over the wrong soldier!'[36]

As Twain pursued his literary career in San Francisco, he and Steve Gillis continued to live together, though they had traded their luxurious accommodations at the Occidental Hotel for the modest comfort Steve's parents offered them. Twain got to know the whole family, including Steve's brothers and sisters. Some nights Twain would accompany him to one beer joint or another on Montgomery Street. Whereas Twain enjoyed 'a restful, pleasant time' at the saloon, Steve Gillis used to pick fights with strangers for fun. When they were not out drinking, Twain typically kept his nose stuck in a book. His devotion to literature impressed Gillis. 'I never knew Sam Clemens to be without a book to study,' he recalled. Twain, in turn, was impressed with Gillis's willingness to help those in need.[37]

Walking down Howard Street one night, Gillis passed Big Jim Casey's saloon to witness the despicable proprietor pummelling the last customer of the night. Interceding on the barfly's behalf, Gillis separated the two. Once the man fled, Casey directed his rage toward Gillis. Unfazed, Gillis hefted an empty beer pitcher and smashed it on Big Jim's head, knocking him to the floor. The police arrested Gillis and charged him with assault and battery. The court set bail at $500.[38]

Since Twain put up the 10 per cent necessary to spring his friend from jail, he fumed when Gillis decided to jump bail and return to Virginia City. Twain would be on the hook for the whole $500. Gillis calmed Twain down and suggested that he could hide out with his brothers Jim and Billy in the mountains. Though Steve Gillis did not realize it at the time, by consigning his friend to his brothers' care, he created an encounter that would help define Mark Twain's literary career.

3

The View from Jackass Hill

Jim Gillis, who was in San Francisco when Mark Twain needed
to get out, welcomed him to stay in the cabin on Jackass Hill in
Tuolumne County he shared with his brother Billy and their friend
Dick Stoker. Named for an animal symbolizing humility and
patience, Jackass Hill proved to be a good place for Twain to bide
his time. In his autobiography he situates the Gillis cabin in a
'serene and reposeful and dreamy and delicious sylvan paradise'.
Written forty years after the fact, these words sound like Twain
idealizing his personal past, but he also captured the region's
natural grandeur in a contemporary notebook entry after
witnessing a lunar rainbow one night. His time on Jackass Hill
gave him a dual pleasure: scenic beauty and good fellowship.[1]

Twain got along well with all three men. Like their brother Steve,
Jim and Billy Gillis were 'made of grit'. Stoker, as Twain caricatured
him in *Roughing It*, was 'gray as a rat, earnest, thoughtful, slenderly
educated, slouchily dressed and clay-soiled, but his heart was finer
metal than any gold his shovel ever brought to light'. The three
were pocket miners, had been for years. A precarious way to make
a living, pocket mining required an eagle eye but little capital outlay.
It involved searching for rich spots or 'pockets' of gold-bearing
quartz, which could be discerned from the surface.[2]

A graduate of the Botanico-Medical College in Memphis,
Tennessee, Jim Gillis was trained as a practitioner of herbal
medicine, but the pocket miner's laidback lifestyle held an

irresistible allure. A friend observed, 'When there was no necessity to labor he loved to loaf and read. He loved books, and his range of reading was wide and his taste cultivated.' Twain noticed Shakespeare and Dickens on Jim's bookshelf. Dan De Quille called pocket miners 'the "Bohemians" of the mining world' and considered Jim 'the Thoreau of the Sierras', not only for his simple life in a wilderness cabin and his voracious reading, but for his knowledge of natural history: 'As a minute observer of every living thing from a pismire to a grizzly bear he out Thoreaus Thoreau – leaves him miles behind.'[3]

Twain recognized another aspect of Jim Gillis's personality: he was a master storyteller. He could have succeeded as a platform lecturer, but Gillis had no desire to trade his seat at the fireplace to stand behind a podium. Gifted with 'a bright and smart imagination', he continually improvised, piling details on details regardless where the story went. He typically made Stoker his subject. Everything that happens in his stories, Jim would assert, really happened to Dick Stoker.[4]

Jim's storytelling technique significantly influenced Twain, who would incorporate tales he heard on Jackass Hill in *Roughing It*,

Gillis Cabin, Jackass Hill, Tuolumne County, California, undated, photographic print.

Carol M. Highsmith, *Angel's Camp, California's Most Famous Gold Rush Town*, 2012, photograph.

Adventures of Huckleberry Finn and *A Tramp Abroad*. Chapter 61 of *Roughing It* uses a structure common to many stories in the Old Southwest tradition. It begins in Mark Twain's voice, but in the third paragraph his inside narrator, Dick Baker, takes over. Twain's Dick Baker, a version of Gillis's Dick Stoker, tells the story of Tom Quartz, a beloved cat that got caught in a mine shaft and almost lost its life in an explosion.

Lifted from the cabin on Jackass Hill and plonked down in the middle of *Roughing It*, the story of Tom Quartz becomes a fable for modern times, a cautionary tale about greed-driven technology. Tom Quartz, a wonderful, wonderful cat, enjoys pocket mining, an environmentally friendly form of excavation. Only when Dick Baker gets ambitious, starts drilling mine shafts into the earth and placing dynamite in them does Tom Quartz object. Once dynamite almost blows the cat to smithereens, Tom Quartz refuses to have anything more to do with mine shafts. When Twain resumes the outside narrative, he depicts Baker's facial expression as he remembers Tom

Quartz: 'The affection and the pride that lit up Baker's face when he delivered this tribute to the firmness of his humble friend of other days, will always be a vivid memory with me.'[5] Twain's memory is made up: Dick Stoker never had a cat.

'The Tragedy of the Burning Shame', a Jim Gillis yarn Twain adapted for *Huckleberry Finn*, is based on a traditional story about the bawdy antics of two travelling showmen. Twain called it 'one of the most outrageously funny things' he had ever heard. Dick Stoker contributed to the hilarity by playing Rinaldo, a principal character. Transferring the story to *Huckleberry Finn*, Twain put the king and the duke into the roles of the two travelling showmen and softened its salacious details. He later exclaimed, 'How mild it is in the book, and how pale; how extravagant and how gorgeous in its unprintable form!'[6]

Assuming Huckleberry Finn's voice, John Seelye has filled in some details Twain omitted. After working up the audience's expectations, the duke raises the curtain:

The next minute the king comes a-prancing out on all fours, naked; and he was painted all over, ring-streaked-and-striped, all sorts of colors, as splendid as a rainbow, but the wildest part of his outfit was a lit candle that was stuck upright in his ass. Well, it was outrageous, but it was awful derned funny. The people most killed themselves laughing.[7]

In the fourth week of January Twain ascended to Angel's Camp in Calaveras County with Jim Gillis, who had a mining claim there. Cold rain kept them and other miners indoors huddled around a wood stove swapping yarns by the score. Twain listened to them enthralled, later filling his notebook with what he had heard. In addition to Gillis's stories, Twain heard a knee-slapper about a gambling man with a high-flying pet frog. Once the rain let up and they went outside to work the claim, the jumping frog story continued to give him and Jim Gillis chuckles. They remembered and repeated it while they worked.[8]

Twain descended from Angel's Camp the last week of February, returning to San Francisco a new man, having reinforced his confidence in the powers of the vernacular to inspire great writing. He resumed his journalistic career where he had left off, contributing further sketches to the *Californian* and placing more articles with local magazines. In addition he strengthened his Nevada connections, becoming San Francisco correspondent for the *Enterprise.* Another literary opportunity came from Artemus Ward, who had written to ask Twain for a sketch to include in his forthcoming book, *Artemus Ward, His Travels.* In his reply Twain mentioned the frog tale but wondered whether he could finish writing it in time. Ward wrote back and encouraged him to finish the story and send it directly to his publisher, George W. Carleton, to expedite its publication.

Before writing 'The Celebrated Jumping Frog of Calaveras County', Twain rehearsed the story orally. When Bret Harte heard him tell it, Twain 'half unconsciously dropped into the lazy tone and manner of the original narrator'.[9] He understood that capturing the storyteller's voice was the key to telling the tale, but it took him months to get it right.

Organizing the work as a frame tale let him begin the outside narrative in the voice of Mark Twain before the inside narrator, Simon Wheeler, takes control. In his first attempt the outside narrative continues for five pages but never does get to the inside narrative. In his second the outside narrator stops short, never properly setting up the story. In 'Jim Smiley and His Jumping Frog', as Twain titled the completed story upon its initial publication, the ratio is just right.

'Jim Smiley and His Jumping Frog' possesses another framing device. Twain wrote it as a personal letter to Artemus Ward, complete with salutation and closing. After mentioning the story, Twain describes Simon Wheeler and the bar room where he found him. He also mentions how Wheeler told the story: 'To me, the spectacle of a man drifting serenely along through such a queer yarn without ever smiling was exquisitely absurd.'[10] Or so he says. In truth Wheeler's storytelling manner represents the deadpan style Sam learned from his mother. The closing frame is quite short. After hearing the story Twain attempts to leave, but Wheeler starts describing Smiley's 'yaller one-eyed cow', at which point Twain interrupts him, says goodbye and clears out.

Twain finished 'Jim Smiley and His Jumping Frog' in the third week of October and sent it directly to Carleton. As he feared, the story arrived too late to appear in *Artemus Ward, His Travels*, but Carleton passed it along to *Saturday Press*. When 'Jim Smiley and His Jumping Frog' appeared in the 18 November 1865 issue, it 'set all New York in a roar'.[11] New Yorkers were not the only readers who roared with laughter. Papers across the nation reprinted the story. In a headnote to one hitherto unrecorded reprint, the Cleveland *Daily Leader* recognized the importance of Twain's time among the California miners:

'Mark Twain' is as well known on the Pacific side of the Rocky Mountains as a humorous writer, as Artemus Ward on this side. His chief *forte* appears to be his complete familiarity with the idioms of California miners and roughs, and his keen appreciation of the ludicrous in them.[12]

The same day *Saturday Press* published 'Jim Smiley and His Jumping Frog', the *Californian* published 'The Launch of the Steamer *Capital*', Twain's spoof of the 'inevitable old platitudinal trash' that typically accompanied such events as the launch of a new steamboat.[13] He chose to tell this story as a frame tale, as well. In the outside narrative Twain relates how he and Muff Nickerson boarded a steamer bound for the launch site and then headed toward the bar room, where they began swapping stories. Eventually Twain hands the narrative to Nickerson, who tells a story about a showman who travelled around the country displaying a panorama painted with episodes from the Bible.

Unlike Simon Wheeler, Nickerson eschews a deadpan style, taking great delight in his details. Describing the audience at a panorama show one night, he says how the 'young bucks and heifers' enjoy the panorama 'because it gives them a chance to taste one another's mugs in the dark'.[14] By the time Nickerson's story ends, he and Twain have completely missed the launch. The telling of a great story, Twain implies, is a worthier event than the launch of the latest steamship.

His growing renown elicited numerous offers from other newspapers. The most appealing one came from the Sacramento *Union*, which invited him to take a four-month journey to the Sandwich Islands (Hawaii). Twain's Hawaiian letters helped sharpen his travel-writing skills. They do not display the narrative sureness that *Innocents Abroad* would demonstrate a few years later, but they do show their author experimenting with different narrative strategies.

To enliven his travels, Twain invented a fictional travelling companion named Mr Brown. Decadent and self-indulgent, Brown reincarnates the Unreliable from Twain's Nevada days. He is a loud-mouthed traveller unafraid to speak his mind, to say whatever pops into his head no matter how inappropriate or uncouth. Like the Unreliable, Brown is a surrogate for Twain who expresses what Tony Tanner calls 'the vulgarity, impudence, uninhibitedness and genuine protest active in a part of his own mind'.[15]

Describing their departure from San Francisco, Twain illustrates Mr Brown's decadence, which manifests itself in his capacity for strong drink, something he shares with many other passengers aboard their Honolulu-bound vessel:

We backed out from San Francisco at 4 p.m., all full – some full of tender regrets for severed associations, others full of buoyant anticipations of a pleasant voyage and a revivifying change of scene, and yet others full of schemes for extending their business relations and making larger profits. The balance were full of whiskey. All except Brown. Brown had had a couple of peanuts for lunch, and therefore one could not say he was full of whiskey, solely, without shamefully transcending the limits of truth.[16]

As this passage illustrates, the character of Mr Brown let Mark Twain tightly control the story, maintaining his narrative distance and using well-balanced and finely crafted sentences to describe what, in plain terms, amounted to a boatload of drunks. While Twain soberly observes the action, Brown abandons himself to the moment and joins the fun.

In Hawaii Twain foresaw what his contemporary readers wanted. Everyone or every man, at least, longed to know more about the hula, the seductive, semi-nude dance that let Hawaiians honour their deities. Upon mentioning 'the lascivious dance that was wont to set the passions of men ablaze in the old heathen days', Twain sounds like he might set ablaze the passions of modern man. As soon as the hula dancers begin their undulations, however, they voice 'the most unearthly caterwauling that was ever heard'.[17] Suddenly, titillation yields to grotesquery. Twain's hula dancers demonstrate another narrative strategy he would often employ, establishing one set of expectations and then undercutting it, giving readers something completely different from what he had led them to expect.

Twain returned to San Francisco from Hawaii in August and prepared a lecture on the subject. His advertising slogan for the event was a stroke of genius: 'Doors open at half past 7, the trouble begins at 8.'[18] Delivered to a sold-out crowd, his lecture was a rousing success, which he used to launch a lecture tour across northern California and Nevada. Twain ended his tour in Virginia City, where he also caught up with old friends.

William Barstow had the most news. He had married 'an educated, cultivated lady' full of vim who had come to Nevada as a schoolteacher. By Twain's return in 1866, the Barstows had already welcomed their first child into the world. When Twain lived in Virginia City, he had known Barstow's bride-to-be well enough to call her 'Kitty'. Joe Goodman also knew her, which did not mean he liked her. Never hesitant to cut through the treacle to say how he saw things, Goodman called Kitty Barstow a 'succubus'.[19]

It was good to see Goodman and the gang at the *Enterprise*, but, in terms of his writing career, Twain found little to keep him in Virginia City or, for that matter, in San Francisco. It was time he moved on. Less than two weeks after returning to San Francisco, he boarded the *America* on the first leg of his journey to New York. He would use his departure in the conclusion to *Roughing It*, telling readers how he left 'the friendliest land and livest, heartiest community on our continent'.[20] Before leaving, Twain received a roving commission with the *Alta California*, which let him travel wherever he wished, reporting his adventures to the newspaper. He had much to report in his initial dispatch. On 15 December 1866, his first night out of San Francisco, the *America* nearly capsized.

Twain's storm at sea ranks among the best in American literature. His portrayal of the ship being tossed by the waves like a plaything is common enough. So is his image of the ship balancing on the crest of a huge wave before plunging into the gulf on the other side. Twain supplies originality by creating a sideways force. As the *America* balances atop one wave and the passengers anticipate its downward plunge, another wave suddenly attacks from the side and sends the ship 'stunned and staggering, broadside on, like a man struck with a club!'[21] Twain's personification brings the passage alive. He takes words commonly associated with a San Francisco bar fight and makes them suit the forces of nature.

The *America* survived the storm largely through Captain Ned Wakeman's quick thinking. At the helm of the *America* Wakeman demonstrated what a good skipper he was. In conversation with Twain he demonstrated what a good storyteller he was. During the voyage the two became friends. Twain supplied a fine character sketch of him in his autobiography, which begins:

> He was a great, burly, handsome, weatherbeaten, symmetrically built and powerful creature, with coal black hair and whiskers, and the kind of eye which men obey without talking back. He was full of human nature, and the best kind of human nature. He was as hearty and sympathetic and loyal and loving a soul as I have found anywhere, and when his temper was up he performed all the functions of an earthquake, without the noise.[22]

Wakeman skippered the *America* safely from San Francisco to San Juan del Sur, Nicaragua, where it arrived on 28 December. After a two-day overland journey across Nicaragua, Twain and his fellow travellers reached Greytown, where they boarded the *San Francisco* for New York. On 2 January 1867, one day out of Greytown, cholera struck. Within the week three passengers were dead, a fourth almost so. In fear for their lives, many disembarked at Key West. Twain took his chances aboard the *San Francisco*. By the time it entered New York harbour on 12 January, seven people had died. Upon disembarking, Twain checked into the Metropolitan Hotel, a luxurious six-storey brownstone on the northeast corner of Broadway and Prince Street, where visitors from California typically stayed.

In New York Twain began living the literary life, seeking to fulfil some of his writerly ambitions. His quest to publish an illustrated edition of his Hawaiian dispatches proved unsuccessful. He also hoped to issue a selected edition of his tales and sketches. Furthermore, he wanted to lecture in New York and possibly elsewhere but hesitated to do so hastily. And he sought a New York magazine that would pay well for regular contributions. All these tasks proved more difficult than expected, especially when his business required him to traipse through the streets of the city during a savage winter.

Charles Henry Webb, who had reached New York several months earlier, helped make Twain's life easier. Webb was living on Broadway a few blocks north of the Metropolitan Hotel, and the two men reunited within days of Twain's arrival. Already Webb had established himself at the centre of a circle of New York journalists, a group that included Edward H. 'Ned' House, the music critic of the *Tribune* who, in Twain's words, had 'a mobile, animated, and brightly intellectual face, and most charming and engaging manners'.[23] As they spoke, Webb encouraged Twain to publish a collection of periodical pieces and agreed to help. Twain had a scrapbook of clippings containing his finest tales and sketches. Twain said Webb was the one who selected and edited the works that went into the published collection, typically downplaying the effort he put into the work himself.

Twain thought it made good sense to approach George W. Carleton, who had a reputation for publishing American comic writers. At Carleton's bookstore and publishing house on Broadway, Twain had difficulty making it past the man outside the office door. When he finally breached the inner office, Carleton greeted him brusquely. In Twain's autobiography Carleton expands to monstrous proportions once the author of 'Jumping Frog' offers him the manuscript:

> He began to swell, and went on swelling and swelling and swelling until he had reached the dimensions of a god of about the second or third degree. Then the fountains of his great deep were broken up, and for two or three minutes I couldn't see him for the rain. It was words, only words, but they fell so densely

that they darkened the atmosphere. Finally he made an imposing sweep with his right hand which comprehended the whole room and said,

'Books – look at those shelves! Every one of them is loaded with books that are waiting for publication. Do I want any more? Excuse me, I don't. Good morning.'[24]

Carleton himself told the story differently. He said that he turned down Twain's manuscript 'because the author looked so disreputable'. Rejected by Carleton, regardless of why, Twain was in good company: earlier that decade Carleton had turned down Herman Melville's first book of poetry.[25]

Webb subsequently agreed to publish *The Celebrated Jumping Frog of Calaveras County, and Other Sketches*. This, the first book he published, is Webb's greatest contribution to literary history. Besides publishing the collection, he also wrote its preface, which reinforces Twain's reputation as the 'Wild Humorist of the Pacific Slope'. The book appeared on 30 April 1867.[26]

Earlier that month George Washington Harris had published *Sut Lovingood Yarns Spun by a 'Nat'ral Born Durn'd Fool'*, a collection of sketches that forms an outstanding example of Old Southwest humour. Though Twain had read many of these sketches when they originally appeared in the newspapers, he added the book to his personal library. He mentions it in a letter to the *Alta California*: 'The book abounds in humor, and is said to represent the Tennessee dialect correctly. It will sell well in the West, but the Eastern people will call it coarse and possibly taboo it.'[27]

Twain's remarks reflect the uneasiness he felt towards an important literary progenitor. He admired Harris's ability to capture the Tennessee dialect and wanted very much to attempt something similar, to do for Missouri what Harris had done for Tennessee, that is, to master the various spoken dialects in his writing. On the other hand, Twain worried that an author of humorous dialect stories would be effectively barred from a refined Eastern readership and thus denied both income and reputation.

Despite his fears, *The Celebrated Jumping Frog of Calaveras County and Other Sketches* was greeted enthusiastically. Many reviewers praised Twain's humour. The most perceptive ones saw something more. The *New-York Citizen*, for instance, observed that Twain's 'chief characteristic is his habit of bringing two utterly incongruous things in close juxtaposition'.[28] Some readers liked other items in the collection better than the title story. The *Philadelphia Inquirer* preferred 'The Killing of Julius Caesar "Localized"', finding it 'infinitely superior' to 'Jumping Frog'. Not all the reviews were positive. Another Philadelphia reader found Twain's tales and sketches 'so forced and strained as to be unnatural'.[29]

Twain timed his first lecture in New York to follow on the heels of *The Celebrated Jumping Frog*. He booked the Cooper Institute for Monday, 6 May 1867, and his inaugural New York lecture proved a rousing success. The New York correspondent of the *Anglo-American Times* applauded Twain's 'brilliant and eloquent lecture' and appended a brief appreciation of the book, concluding that *The Celebrated Jumping Frog* 'places its author in the colour-guard of American humorists'.[30]

George Routledge, a London publisher who had made his fortune pirating American books for the British market, issued *The Celebrated Jumping Frog of Calaveras County, and Other Sketches* in September 1867. Inexpensively produced and priced at a shilling, the book could be found in railway bookstalls and corner bookshops across Great Britain. The Routledge edition sold more copies in Britain than Webb's edition sold in the United States. Twain earned nothing from the pirated British edition, which initiated his longstanding campaign for international copyright legislation.

British reviewers welcomed *The Celebrated Jumping Frog*. The *London Review* favourably compared Mark Twain to Artemus Ward. Twain avoided Ward's clever misspellings and tricks of dialect to achieve his comic effects: 'Mark Twain shows that he can amuse the public single-handed and without costume, as effectively as if he dressed as a showman and talked through his nose.'[31] Assuming the persona of an ignorant showman, Artemus Ward had limited his potential by confining himself to his fictional identity. In contrast, the witty and insightful persona of Mark Twain gave its author almost limitless possibilities.[32] Sadly, Artemus Ward, a victim of tuberculosis, had passed away a few months before *The Celebrated Jumping Frog* appeared. His humorous writings did not long survive him. The publication of Twain's first book sounded the death knell of Artemus Ward.

Thomas Hood reviewed *The Celebrated Jumping Frog* for *Fun*, the humorous weekly he edited, calling it 'one of the funniest books that we have met with for a long time'. British readers were often shocked but nonetheless fascinated to see what Americans had done to the English language. Hood especially liked the part in 'The Launch of the Steamer *Capital*' about the young 'bucks and heifers . . . tasting one another's mugs in the dark'. After overviewing the book's contents, Hood concluded with reference to a character from *The Old Curiosity Shop:*

> Our advice to our readers, therefore, is immediately to invest a shilling in it, and over a pipe and what Mr Swiveller called a 'modest quencher', to sit down and have the hearty laugh that we can promise them from its perusal.[33]

Hood continued to champion Twain's writings. Two years later he upbraided an American author for asserting that his writings were unknown in England. *The Celebrated Jumping Frog*, Hood explained, 'has been on every bookstall for a year and more', and 'his writings have been popular at Penny Readings'.[34]

Organized by community leaders in towns and villages throughout Great Britain, penny readings were designed to elevate the working classes. These events got people out of the pubs, giving them an evening's entertainment for a penny. Usually hosted by the local vicar or the grammar-school headmaster, penny readings were designed to bring quality music and literature to the masses. A typical programme included vocal and instrumental music and readings from respectable literary works.[35]

With the release of the Routledge edition, 'The Celebrated Jumping Frog' became a popular feature of the penny readings. One autumn evening in the Leicestershire village of Kibworth, for example, the vicar and his wife performed a duet for flute and piano. After a few vocal numbers and a reading from Byron's 'The Dream', James Smeeton, a local resident, read 'The Celebrated Jumping Frog', which 'met with a hearty reception'.[36]

Similar events occurred in the antipodes. Towns throughout Australia hosted 'popular readings', which also included vocal and instrumental performances by local musicians. After George Robertson – the John Murray of Australia – published the Melbourne edition of *The Celebrated Jumping Frog of Calaveras County, and Other Sketches*, its contents entered the repertoire for popular readings. For the last popular reading of 1868 in Myrniong, Victoria, a town 40 miles northwest of Melbourne, one Mr Harbord read 'Jumping Frog' to great acclaim. The correspondent for the *Bacchus Marsh Express* reported that Twain's story 'was rendered in good style, and caused much merriment'.[37]

New Zealand had its own popular readings, which were called 'winter readings' or 'winter evening entertainments'. One Friday night at the Colonists' Hall in Lyttelton, a town just south of Christchurch, H. S. Bolt read 'Jumping Frog', which 'caused great laughter'. Much further south, at the town hall in Clyde, another winter reading also included 'Jumping Frog' on the programme.[38]

Though 'Jumping Frog' was Twain's most popular work at these readings, performers occasionally read other pieces from the collection. In Kaiapoi, a New Zealand town near Christchurch,

Captain Morgan, an American visitor, read 'A Touching Story of George Washington's Boyhood', which was so highly acclaimed that he read 'Jumping Frog' as an encore. In Cheltenham, England, the Cotswold Rifle Corps organized a penny reading for the local community. Ensign Packwood read 'A Touching Story of George Washington's Boyhood'. According to the *Cheltenham Chronicle*, Packwood 'failed to impart the humorous manner to it which would have made it as successful as it might have been, the subject was lively, but the reading was somewhat too solemn'. In Heathcote, Victoria, R. C. Carkeet read 'Curing a Cold': 'He read very distinctly, but failed to enter into the fun of the subject himself or lead his hearers there.'[39] Since the performers were local amateurs, occasional shortcomings could be expected. By no means did they diminish the popularity of the readings, which would grow for decades, thanks, in no small part, to Twain's early writings. *The Celebrated Jumping Frog of Calaveras County* introduced Mark Twain to the world.

4

The Innocents Abroad

Learning about an upcoming luxury cruise from New York through Europe to the Near East, Mark Twain saw the five-month excursion as an ideal way to continue his newspaper correspondence, which was growing stale the longer he stayed in New York. Encountering new people in new places would let him entertain the readers of the *Alta California* and form the basis for a new book, *The Innocents Abroad*. The cost of the cruise was exorbitant, but the *Alta* approved Twain's request, and he obtained passage aboard the *Quaker City*.

His instructions were simple: continue submitting regular letters 'in the same style that heretofore secured you the favor of the readers of the *Alta California*'.[1] Though these instructions locked him into a literary style, the persona he had invented offered much flexibility. Having established a reputation for stretching the truth as Mark Twain, he could keep doing so. He also reached agreements to contribute signed articles to the New York *Tribune* and unsigned ones to the New York *Herald*.

Moses Sperry Beach – publisher of the New York *Sun* – and his seventeen-year-old daughter Emma hosted a reception for their fellow passengers on 6 June 1867. Twain's reputation as a humorist preceded him, and his witty banter kept the reception lively. From his perspective, the others were a pile of stuffed shirts, but he made a few friends among them. Emma Beach became a favourite. Daniel Slote – 'Dan' in *The Innocents Abroad* – would be his cabinmate aboard the *Quaker City*. At 39 Slote was closer in age to Twain than many other passengers. A business executive, he was a senior partner at Slote & Woodman, a blank-book and stationery manufacturer in New York. Knowing his mother worried about the company he kept, Twain teased her: 'I have got a splendid, immoral, tobacco-smoking, wine-drinking, godless room-mate who is as good and true and right-minded a man as ever lived.'[2]

Dr Abraham Reeves Jackson, the fun-loving ship's surgeon, also befriended Twain. Most of those who made it into *The Innocents Abroad* did so as caricatures, but 'The Doctor' in the book closely resembles the original. Jack Van Nostrand, whom Twain privately called a 'long-legged, simple, green, wide-mouthed, horse-laughing young fellow', eventually won him over.[3] And Charlie Langdon, a seventeen-year-old from Elmira, New York, whose father Jervis Langdon, a coal and lumber baron, had sent him on this cruise, became friends with Twain towards the journey's end.

On Saturday morning, 8 June, passengers started boarding the *Quaker City*. In *The Innocents Abroad* Twain says, 'All was bustle and confusion. (I have seen that remark before, somewhere.)' A master of parentheses, Twain follows his cliché with a parenthetical comment, demonstrating how he could transfer his deadpan manner to the written word. By modifying the cliché, the comment shows one way Twain renewed the English language. He often put clichés in his writing only to revitalize them. Describing his well-appointed portside cabin on the *Quaker City*, he observes, 'Notwithstanding all this furniture, there was still room to turn around in, but not to swing a cat in, at least not with entire security to the cat.'[4]

The *Quaker City* pulled away from its slip that afternoon, leaving behind one indecisive passenger, Bloodgood H. Cutter, a wealthy eccentric who fancied himself a poet, though he had a shaky grasp of metre and often wrenched his syntax to make his rhymes. Rain accompanied by gale-force winds beset the *Quaker City*, keeping it in New York harbour for two nights. As it left the harbour Monday

Daniel Slote, engraving, from Mark Twain, *The Innocents Abroad, or The New Pilgrims' Progress* (1870), p. 288.

morning, a boat came crashing through the surf. It carried Cutter, who had finally decided to join the excursion. The model for the 'Poet Lariat' in *The Innocents Abroad*, Cutter would chronicle the journey in verse.[5]

Once the *Quaker City* reached the high seas, the results were predictable. Everyone was afflicted with *nausea marina*, everyone, that is, except the doctor and the former riverboat pilot. The irrepressible Bloodgood Cutter refused to let seasickness get him down. With all its 'plunge and reel', he said, the ship would 'Sometimes makes me quite qualmish feel; / Then I rush to the vessel's side / And heave up in the briny tide.'[6]

Having spent several years in the easy-going American West, Twain had difficulty adjusting to the straight-laced Easterners aboard the *Quaker City*. Most enjoyed prayer meetings and psalm singing too much to suit him. Happily a few shared his passion for euchre, a fast-paced game that could 'strengthen the mind'.[7] Playing euchre let them kill countless hours across the Atlantic. The euchre player's response to a bad hand – 'I pass' – became a catchphrase among the card-playing passengers.

Twain also enjoyed reading aboard the *Quaker City*. The ship's library was not dissimilar to his Sunday school teacher's bookshelf, but Twain found a few enjoyable volumes. Reading George W. Curtis's travel narrative *The Howadji in Syria* under the stars, Twain would invite Emma Beach to keep him company. Late at night he would read aloud passages from *The Howadji in Syria*, showing Emma how beautiful the English language could be.[8]

The *Quaker City* reached Fayal in the Azores on the 21st. Twain reported their stay in detail, even telling readers how to pronounce the city's name: 'The people there pronounce it Fy-all, and put the accent on the first syllable.'[9] In his family correspondence Twain often explains how to pronounce strange place names. Twain's keys to pronunciation verify his keen ear, meticulous nature and crucial understanding of the relationship between language and place. From his early sketches through *Huckleberry Finn*, he would work hard to transfer the spoken language to the written word, capturing subtle nuances of pronunciation and meaning.

The Quaker City in a Storm, engraving, frontispiece to Mark Twain, *The Innocents Abroad, or The New Pilgrims' Progress* (1870).

Port of Horta, Fayal, engraving, from Mark Twain, *The Innocents Abroad, or The New Pilgrims' Progress* (1870), facing p. 56.

On Saturday, 29 June, the *Quaker City* reached Gibraltar, where it would spend two nights. Twain, Slote, Jackson and a few others took a steamer to Tangier, where Twain found the exotic setting he sought. The city's unique mix of people, combined with their unusual dress and strange customs, fascinated him. Before leaving Tangier, they visited the bazaar and, anticipating a fancy dress ball aboard the *Quaker City*, obtained some 'full, flowing, picturesque Moorish costumes'.[10] Their costumes did not seem so picturesque to Bloodgood Cutter, whose eyes on them 'did glance / As with the ladies they did dance.' Cutter concluded that the baggy garments, which the men wore without hose, more nearly resembled their 'night clothes'.[11]

Two days later the Fourth of July offered the American passengers another chance for festivities. They celebrated the Fourth during the day; that night the *Quaker City* reached Marseilles. The passengers scattered in different directions to explore Europe. Many would not return to the ship until it reached Naples a month later. Twain, Jackson and Slote boarded the northbound night train. The Paris Exhibition, supposedly one of the cruise's great attractions, left

Twain cold. For him the highlight of Paris was the parade featuring Napoleon III, who represented 'modern civilization, progress, and refinement'.[12] For readers of *The Innocents Abroad* the highlight of Paris is the guided tour 'Ferguson' gives Twain and his companions. There is a reason why this episode is so good: Twain made it up.

Jackson, Slote and Twain returned to Marseilles on the 12th, reboarded the *Quaker City* and two days later reached Genoa, disembarking to tour Italy overland. The three took the train from Genoa to Milan, where they saw *The Last Supper*. Leonardo's famous fresco did not inspire Twain:

> It is battered and scarred in every direction, and stained and discolored by time, and Napoleon's horses kicked the legs off most of the disciples when they (the horses, not the disciples,) were stabled there more than half a century ago.[13]

View of a Street in Tangier, engraving, from Mark Twain, *The Innocents Abroad, or The New Pilgrims' Progress* (1870), p. 77.

Twain's Italy parallels his Paris: the funniest episodes are those he invented. One day their chatty coachman points out an iron hook attached to a ruined tower and tells them the seven-hundred-year-old legend of Count Luigi, which ends with the count hanging his wicked brother by the chin from the hook for a couple of years. The legend elicits a facetious question: 'Is he dead?'[14]

The text does not indicate which of the three asked the question, the Doctor most likely. In *The Innocents Abroad* the Doctor usually speaks with their guides because he can keep a straight face and 'throw more imbecility into the tone of his voice than any man that lives'.[15] Subsequently they take turns asking the question, which becomes a running gag responsible for several hilarious moments.

Wicked Brother, engraving, from Mark Twain, *The Innocents Abroad, or The New Pilgrims' Progress* (1870), p. 215.

The humour in *The Innocents Abroad* often has a serious purpose: to destroy Romantic notions about the Old World. Venice receives similar treatment. Twain compares it with 'an overflowed Arkansas town' and imagines the water will soon fall and 'leave a dirty high-water mark on the houses, and the streets full of mud and rubbish'.[16] Twain's riverboat background inspired his comparison, letting him convey a distinctly American view. American travellers have often interpreted the Old World by comparing it with the New, no matter how incongruous or insulting the comparison.

From Venice the three travelled through Florence and Pisa to Leghorn, where the *Quaker City* awaited. They boarded the ship but did not stay long. Hearing rumours that a cholera quarantine would prevent them from disembarking at Naples – and thus from seeing Rome – many disembarked at Leghorn and travelled to Naples by other means. Twain, Slote and Jackson took a steamer to Civitavecchia and then proceeded overland.

In Rome they met Richard Garvey, a young Irish-American traveller then living on the Via Babuino who showed them around. In *The Innocents Abroad* Twain does not mention Garvey, whose significance has just recently come to light.[17] His absence from the book reflects its author's creative method. Personal guides triggered Twain's imagination during his travels, prompting him to invent a series of fictional guides oblivious to the antics of Twain and friends. Garvey could have been the one who showed them the Coliseum, the Catacombs or the Capuchin Convent, but Twain created different guides for *The Innocents Abroad*. In the Capuchin Convent a monk shows them some of his predecessors who have been dead for decades and left to mummify in plain sight. As they see one with its greyish skin growing tight across the skull, Twain rushes Dan and the Doctor away before either can ask, 'Is he dead?'

From Rome, they proceeded to Naples, where the *Quaker City* was anchored in the bay with its quarantine flag flying. Bloodgood Cutter's ongoing indecisiveness adversely affected his holiday. He

Engraving of Bloodgood H. Cutter, from Bloodgood H. Cutter, *The Long Island Farmer's Poems: Lines Written on the Quaker City Excursion to Palestine, and Other Poems* (1886).

often stayed with the ship only to regret his decision. Usually he could find good in anything, but knowing that fellow passengers were ashore enjoying Naples while he and a few others were stuck aboard the quarantined ship raised his hackles. He wrote an eleven-stanza verse petition to local health authorities expressing how unfair the situation was:

> And they have left that sickly Rome,
> And in your city they have come;
> And with you there they now do stay,
> While you imprison us in your Bay.[18]

Those in Naples would not reboard the *Quaker City* until it was ready to depart. Twain used the time to catch up his correspondence. William M. Stewart had written to offer him a private secretaryship. Twain accepted. Since Stewart was now representing Nevada in the U.S. Senate, the secretaryship would take Twain to Washington, where he hoped to have sufficient spare time to continue his literary career.

Once all the passengers reunited at Naples, they boarded the *Quaker City*, which left on Sunday 11 August. At Piraeus another quarantine banned them from disembarking and visiting Greece. Indignant at the possibility of missing Athens, Twain, along with Jackson and two other men, defied the quarantine, sneaked ashore and visited the Acropolis, which did not disappoint. Twain called it 'the noblest ruins we had ever seen – the most elegant, the most graceful, the most imposing'.[19]

For some extravagant episodes in his *Alta* correspondence, Twain again used Mr Brown as his stooge. Revising his *Alta* letters for *The Innocents Abroad*, he softened his writing to give it a wider appeal. He omitted Brown altogether, either changing his name to Blucher or distributing his escapades to other characters. For his story of lunch in Constantinople Twain changed 'Brown' to 'Jack', meaning Jack Van Nostrand. The use of Jack's name suggests that the story, no matter how embellished, had its roots in reality. It is so good it bears repetition, regardless of its veracity:

Jack Van Nostrand, from Mark Twain, *The Innocents Abroad, or The New Pilgrims' Progress* (1870), p. 490.

I never shall want another Turkish lunch. The cooking apparatus was in the little lunch room, near the bazaar, and it was all open to the street. The cook was slovenly, and so was the table, and it had no cloth on it. The fellow took a mass of sausage-meat and coated it round a wire and laid it on a charcoal fire to cook. When it was done, he laid it aside and a dog walked sadly in and nipped it. He smelt it first, and probably recognized the remains of a friend. The cook took it away from him and laid it before us. Jack said, 'I pass' – he plays euchre sometimes – and we all passed in turn. Then the cook baked a broad, flat, wheaten cake, greased it well with the sausage, and started towards us with it. It dropped in the dirt, and he picked it up and polished it on his breeches, and laid it before us. Jack said, 'I pass'. We all passed. He put some eggs in a frying pan, and stood pensively prying slabs of meat from between his teeth with a fork. Then he used the fork to turn the eggs with – and brought them along. Jack said 'Pass again'. All followed suit. We did not know what to do, and so we ordered a new ration of sausage. The cook got out his wire, apportioned a proper amount of sausage-meat, spat it on his hands and fell to work! This time, with one accord, we all passed out. We paid and left. That is all I learned about Turkish lunches. A Turkish lunch is good, no doubt, but it has its little drawbacks.[20]

Despite its side-splitting hilarity, this passage confirms Joe Goodman's theory about the defensive nature of Twain's humour. Throughout *The Innocents Abroad*, Twain reacts to culture and customs different from his own by making fun of them. In Turkey he discovers that people behave differently, have different standards of cleanliness and differ in matters of personal space. Twain cannot adjust his behaviour accordingly but instead makes fun of what he sees, exaggerating it to outrageous proportions.

In Beirut Twain, Slote and others contracted with a dragoman to lead them by horseback to Damascus and then south through

Street Scene in Constantinople, engraving, from Mark Twain, *The Innocents Abroad, or The New Pilgrims' Progress* (1870), facing p. 359.

Palestine to Jerusalem. Twain's disgust with the pilgrims comes to a head during this segment of the trip. Since their dogmatic piety prevents them from travelling on the Sabbath, the rest of the week they must ride their horses almost to death to make up the lost day. Their misplaced piety undermines basic tenets of charity, decency and humanity – aspects more fundamental to Christianity than the Sabbath. Twain observes, 'They were willing to commit a sin against the spirit of religious law, in order that they might preserve the letter of it.'[21]

Jerusalem itself, the centre of the Holy Land, convinces Twain that every place associated with Scripture is a humbug. He walks a tightrope throughout the Holy Land portions of *The Innocents Abroad*. Wanting very much to expose the vulgar errors of religious belief, he can only go so far without offending devout Christian readers, who dominated the American reading public. His notebooks contain additional ideas he omitted from *The Innocents Abroad* in an act of self-censorship: 'Recall infant Christ's pranks on his school-mates – striking boys dead – withering their hands.'[22]

Twain's humour returns to the level of the Turkish lunch when he encounters Adam's tomb:

> How touching it was, here in a land of strangers, far away from home, and friends and all who cared for me, thus to discover the grave of a blood relation. True, a distant one, but still a relation. The unerring instinct of nature thrilled its recognition. The fountain of my filial affection was stirred to its profoundest depths, and I gave way to tumultuous emotion. I leaned upon a pillar and burst into tears. I deem it no shame to have wept over the grave of my poor dead relative.[23]

He continues in this manner for several more sentences, each further exploding the maudlin sentimentalism associated with religious belief, mourning practices and popular travel writing. His words are extraordinary: many readers had never heard anything quite like it. One had. Tabitha Quarles could hear her cousin Sam's voice as she read *The Innocents Abroad*, though she misremembered a detail while recalling the book:

> Shucks, that's just like Sam all over. It is just the way he used to talk and fool about things when he was a boy. Why, that book was the biggest nonsense I ever read. The idea of his standing and weeping over Noah's grave, and stuff like that. But that was the way Sam used to make fun of things when he was a boy.[24]

Egypt was the highlight of the return trip. Leaving Jaffa early on 1 October, the *Quaker City* reached Alexandria at sunset the following day. Twain received some disappointing news at Alexandria: many letters to the *Alta* had miscarried. Since he had not saved copies, he would have to write several unplanned letters during the return trip. Twain refused to let his literary work interfere with his Egyptian travels. With Slote and Van Nostrand, he went by train to Cairo, where they hired donkeys to reach the Sphinx and the pyramids. Otherwise he wrote.

Slote remembered Twain as 'the hardest-working man I ever saw', using his behaviour in Egypt as an example: 'Why, out in Egypt, where the fleas were so thick you couldn't breath without swallowing a thousand, that man used to sit up and write, write, half the night.' Slote also recalled their Egyptian banter.

> 'Sam, how the deuce can you stand it to write out there among the fleas?'
>
> 'Oh, I'm all right', he replied. 'They've got a railroad track eaten out around both ankles, and they keep in that pretty well, so I don't bother with them.'[25]

Back in Alexandria they said their goodbyes. Slote left the excursion to revisit Europe, and the *Quaker City* steamed home.

Twain did not waste time upon reaching New York. The *Quaker City* docked on Tuesday morning, 19 November. That afternoon he visited the newspaper offices to see how his reputation was doing. Learning his *Tribune* letters had been reprinted in newspapers across the country, Twain regretted he had not written more.[26] He had assumed his *Alta* letters would be disseminated out West but was unsure whether they would reach newspaper offices in the East. Twain was mortified to learn the *Alta* had copyrighted the letters: an unusual step. He worried the copyright had prevented them from being reprinted in other newspapers and thus had done nothing to advance his reputation.[27]

His entire correspondence may not have been reprinted, but newspapers across the nation extracted his *Alta* letters. After his dispatch from Constantinople appeared in the *Alta* in October, for instance, his tale of a Turkish lunch was reprinted from Rock Island, Illinois, to Galveston, Texas, to Bangor, Maine. These newspaper reprints were signed 'Mark Twain'; either that or they put his name in their titles.[28] Twain's American reputation was greater now than ever before.

A book offer confirmed his growing renown. When Elisha Bliss Jr, secretary and managing director of the American Publishing Company, a subscription-book house in Hartford, Connecticut, heard about Twain's return, he wrote to offer him a contract. Bliss suggested a volume based on his travels but left the subject to him. Twain replied, expressing his interest and approving its publishing method. Subscription publishing sought new readerships by appealing to people who lived in rural areas or smaller towns without local bookstores.[29]

The key to subscription publishing was the book agent. Publishers like Bliss would recruit desperate yet hardworking men and women to sell books door to door. Annie Nelles, for one, became a book agent after she left her husband upon discovering his bigamy. She was proud to have a career of her own that contributed to the nation's intellectual life by introducing books to homes that had none. Through the efforts of book agents like herself, she said, people who never buy books are 'induced to subscribe for some work of interest and benefit'.[30]

Book agents became so prevalent that people dreaded their sight. Though Twain would build his career on subscription publishing, he nonetheless spoofed the book agent's ubiquity. In 'Burlesque Hamlet' he retells Shakespeare's tragedy by introducing a new character, a book agent named Basil Stockmar, who soliloquizes: 'I do get mighty tired of hearing that same old welcome, always in the same old words, "O, here's another dam *book* agent!"'[31]

The agent canvassed an area with a specimen copy in one hand and a subscription list in the other. When Basil Stockmar reaches Denmark, he carries both a canvassing copy and a subscription list. Publishers also supplied agents with detailed instructions regarding how to pitch a book. Inside his canvassing copy, Basil has written his sales pitch, which he hopes to memorize, knowing it should 'glide off the tongue pretty glib and oily and natural-like . . . to get the best effect and convert the candidate'.[32]

The instructions recommended that agents get the community's most influential citizens to subscribe. Prominently recorded at the front of the list, their names would encourage neighbours to follow suit. When she reached Peoria, Illinois, Annie Nelles initially recruited one prominent businessman and two attorneys, knowing their names would benefit her Peoria canvassing. By persuading the Queen of Denmark and Prince Hamlet to subscribe, Basil Stockmar hopes to recruit additional subscribers.[33]

Subscription books were quite expensive: they had to be to support a vast network of distributors and agents. Marketed to reluctant consumers, the subscription book needed a certain heft: it had to be long enough to seem worth the money, say, five or six hundred pages. Copious illustrations enhanced its entertainment value. In addition consumers could select different bindings at different price points. The basic subscription book was clothbound with an embossed and illustrated cover, but tooled and gilt calf was an option at the high end. Placed in a home with few books, the subscription book was not just something to read, but a showpiece to be displayed prominently on the parlour table.

Its iconic status in the home greatly affected the subscription book's contents. As something for the whole family, the book could not contain anything inappropriate or untoward. Its text had to be suitable for parents and grandparents and children to read aloud together. Upon reading her specimen copy of *Tom Sawyer*, Harriet Wasson, a book agent based in Oakland, California, could tell that 'it was a book intended for youthful minds, and all in reading-life, clean through to the oldest age.'[34]

When Twain first signed with the American Publishing Company, he did not fully realize how subscription publishing would affect his writing. Elisha Bliss would work closely with him to soften text that might challenge its readers' religious beliefs. Some authors balked at how subscription publishing limited their ability to express themselves, but Twain accepted the limitations as the realities of the marketplace. He wanted to make money from his writing and saw little reason to write books unless he could make money doing so.

Twain did not receive the invitation from Bliss until December. By then he had left New York for Washington to assume his position as Senator Stewart's private secretary. Stewart rented rooms at 224 F Street and invited Twain to live with him. Stewart caricatured Twain's appearance in his reminiscences: 'He was arrayed in a seedy suit, which hung upon his lean frame in bunches with no style worth mentioning . . . an evil-smelling cigar butt, very much frazzled, protruded from the corner of his mouth.'[35]

While continuing to write for the *Alta*, Twain reached agreements to maintain a Washington correspondence with the New York *Tribune*, the New York *Herald* and the Virginia City *Enterprise*. The secretaryship, which began in late November, barely lasted into December. His contact with lawmakers in Washington made little impact on his literary reputation, but it did yield one delightful epigram: 'Whiskey is taken into committee rooms in demijohns and carried out in demagogues.'[36]

Since the role of Washington correspondent did not always tie him to the capital, Twain visited New York over the Christmas holidays. One night he and Dan Slote, who had recently returned from Europe, got together with Jack Van Nostrand and Charlie Langdon. Twain recorded the evening in a letter to his mother: 'I just laughed till my sides ached, at some of our reminiscences. It was the unholiest gang that ever cavorted through Palestine.' Jane Clemens seldom enjoyed hearing about her son's wild times, but she liked what he said next. Since Charlie Langdon was in New York with his sister Olivia and their father, Twain visited her on New Year's Day. He told his mother, 'I anchored for the day at the first house I came to – Charlie Langdon's sister was there (beautiful girl).'[37]

Twain's New Year's Day visit marked the second or third time he had met Olivia 'Livy' Langdon. Ten years younger than Twain, she had a waif-like appearance: 'slender and beautiful and girlish'. On New Year's Eve Twain had met the Langdons at their hotel and accompanied them to Steinway Hall to hear Charles Dickens read from *David Copperfield*. Twain recalled: 'His reading of the storm scene in which Steerforth lost his life, was so vivid, and so full of energetic action, that the house was carried off its feet, so to speak.'[38]

Back in Washington the second week of January 1868, Twain started writing *The Innocents Abroad*. Wanting to base the book on his newspaper correspondence, he asked his mother to send whatever *Alta* letters she possessed. Altogether the letters would make only a 250-page book. By the terms of his contract, it needed to be at least five hundred pages.[39] In other words, turning his newspaper correspondence into a book would take twice as much work as it had taken to write the original letters. Twain had much else to write as well. Since Bliss refused to give him an advance, he maintained his Washington correspondence to pay living expenses.

One day Twain took time out from *The Innocents Abroad* to offer Emma Beach some writerly advice:

> To condense the diffused light of a page of thought into the luminous flash of a single sentence, is worthy to rank as a prize composition just by itself . . . *Any*body can have ideas – the difficulty is to express them without squandering a quire of paper on an idea that ought to be reduced to one glittering paragraph.[40]

Twain gave similar advice to another friend, telling her to seek out literary models. To write clean, concise sentences, authors must read clean, concise sentences. He recommended a seventeenth-century classic, Thomas Fuller's *Worthies of England*. Fuller excelled at writing what Twain called 'pemmican sentences': he 'boils an elaborate thought down and compresses it into a single crisp and meaty sentence'.[41]

Read against his own career, Twain's advice indicates the trouble he faced with *The Innocents Abroad*. Having honed his literary skills writing short, highly crafted sketches, he now faced the difficulty of writing a subscription-length book. By the time he finished, *The Innocents Abroad* would contain many glittering paragraphs and pemmican sentences, but it sometimes took pages of expository prose to connect them.

Twain kept living with Stewart after he left his employ but eventually relocated to a boarding house on Indiana Avenue popular with newspaper correspondents. H. J. Ramsdell remembered him living in 'a little back room, with a sheet-iron stove, a dirty, musty carpet of the cheapest description, a bed and two or three common chairs'. The room was 'sour with tobacco smoke', the floor 'littered with newspapers, from which Twain had cut out his letters' along with 'hundreds of pieces of torn manuscripts which had been written and then rejected by the author'.[42]

Though *The Innocents Abroad* progressed through the winter, in the second week of March its author faced potential disaster. Planning to collect his newspaper correspondence themselves, the *Alta* editors refused to grant Twain permission to reuse his letters. Their plan created a twofold problem. It would force him to rewrite his travels from scratch: a daunting prospect. Twain always had difficulty writing something from nothing; he needed a starting point.

The other part of the problem concerns his public image. Twain had written the *Alta* letters in a zesty style suitable for San Francisco readers. Reshaping his newspaper correspondence into *The Innocents Abroad*, he altered his style to suit what he perceived as a more refined East Coast readership. Should the *Alta* book go through, it would reinforce his reputation as the 'Wild Humorist of the Pacific Slope', a reputation he desperately wanted to shake. Twain knew he could convince the *Alta* publishers to drop their plans and grant him permission to use his newspaper correspondence – but he would have to speak with them in person.

The route through Panama remained the most efficient way to reach California before the transcontinental railroad. While in Panama City waiting for the boat to San Francisco, Twain ran into Ned Wakeman. They caught up and swapped stories. Supposedly Wakeman told a whopper about the time he sailed through outer space to heaven. Though the story may have been Twain's invention, Wakeman was the model for the eponymous hero of 'Captain Stormfield's Visit to Heaven', a work Twain would tinker with for decades.

Twain loved being back in San Francisco, and he visited Virginia City, too. This, the longest trip he had taken since the *Quaker City* excursion, let him compare the two journeys. He told a correspondent about his sleigh ride through the Sierras:

> Coming back last night in a snowstorm, the two and a half hours' sleighing (part of the time clear weather and superb moonlight,) was something magnificent – we made ten miles an hour straight along. We had no such thrilling fun in Palestine.[43]

Having brought his manuscript with him, Twain got back to work on *The Innocents Abroad* once he had secured permission to reuse his *Alta* letters. He shared his manuscript with Bret Harte, who read it carefully and provided many useful suggestions. Harte told Twain 'what passages, paragraphs and *chapters* to leave out'.[44] Twain appreciated Harte's advice at the time, but a rift would develop between them in the coming years. The precise nature of their split remains uncertain, but Twain's relationship with Harte follows the same pattern as many Twain friendships. A perceived slight would lead to a grudge, which would grow to enormous proportions, creating an unbridgeable gap and destroying the friendship.

Work on *The Innocents Abroad* progressed so well in San Francisco that Twain foresaw its completion. He envisioned an army of book agents criss-crossing the continent signing up subscribers. He also thought Far East agents should scour English-speaking enclaves in Japan and China. They would. Three years after *The Innocents Abroad* appeared, a contributor to the Shanghai *North China Herald* said, 'Everybody read and laughed over the *Innocents Abroad*.'[45] By the second week of July, Twain had nearly completed his manuscript. Having written more than he needed, he would streamline his text during the voyage to New York. Twain left San Francisco in the second week of July 1868.

By mid-August Twain had delivered the manuscript to Bliss and earned some much-needed rest. He headed for Elmira, where he saw Charlie Langdon again. He enjoyed meeting his adopted sister Susan and her husband Theodore Crane but really came to see their sister Livy. Before leaving Elmira, he confessed his love for her. After a trip to St Louis to visit his mother and sister, Twain reached Hartford the first week of October. He stayed with Bliss, and together they hunkered down to prepare the printer's copy for *The Innocents Abroad*.

The highlight of Twain's Hartford stay was meeting the Reverend Joseph H. Twichell, who would become a lifelong friend. A few years younger than Twain, Twichell, who had rowed for the Yale crew in college and served as chaplain during the Civil War, had since married Harmony Cushman and become associate pastor of Asylum Hill Congregational Church in Hartford. Given Twain's religious scepticism, it may seem odd that he would become good friends with a preacher, but Twichell was no ordinary preacher. Far from being a strict doctrinaire, Twichell took a broad view of the Bible, interpreting it with thoughtful intelligence. He also had a lively sense of humour. Twain liked to rehearse his ideas orally; Twichell liked to listen.

Winter was the time platform lecturers made their money. Twain went on the lecture circuit during the 1868–9 season. His speech in

Toledo – the city Petroleum V. Nasby called home – on 20 January 1869 was the tour's high point. Afterwards he wrote to Livy:

> It was splendid, to-night – the great hall was crowded full of the pleasantest and handsomest people, and I did the *very best* I possibly could – and did better than I ever did before – I felt the importance of the occasion, for I knew that, this being Nasby's residence, every person in the audience would be comparing and contrasting me with him – and I am satisfied with the performance.[46]

The Toledo papers applauded Twain's lecture. *The Blade*, for one, found him 'irresistibly funny', but recognized he could also deliver 'most eloquent passages, brilliant in thought and word'.[47] R. W. Bliss, who operated the Toledo branch of the American Publishing Company, apparently forwarded the *Blade* review to the home office. Elisha Bliss would reprint it on the cover of an advertising circular for *The Innocents Abroad*.

Upon finishing his lecture tour in March, Twain returned to Hartford to polish *The Innocents Abroad* further. Nasby, then nearing the end of his own lecture tour, soon reached Hartford. Twain attended his lecture, and Nasby came to his rooms afterwards. Together they sat up and talked until dawn. Twain learned, among other things, that Nasby had missed his connection. To reach Hartford in time he had travelled all day and most of the night in a cattle car. 'He had the constitution of an ox and the strength and endurance of a prize-fighter,' Twain said. After their all-night bull session he told Livy, 'I took a strong liking to this fellow, who has some very noble qualities I do assure you, and I did *want* to talk.'[48]

During the summer of 1869 the American Publishing Company began advertising for agents to sell *The Innocents Abroad*. In Defiance, Ohio, for example, an advertisement in the local newspaper described it as 'the most readable, enjoyable, laughable, and popular book

Petroleum Nasby, *c.* 1870, photographic print.

printed for years' and asked potential agents, 'Do you want to make money faster than ever before in your life? Sell this book.'[49]

Similar advertisements appeared elsewhere. One caught Kitty Barstow's attention. Since Twain had seen them, the Barstows had left Virginia City, Nevada, for Fredericksburg, Virginia. They now had three children. William Barstow, who had been working for the u.s. Census Bureau, had lost his position after being charged with a crime. Though he was acquitted, the charge blackened his reputation and he could not find work. Kitty wrote to Twain to secure a book agency for herself. Though Twain had been friends with him, her husband William Barstow's inability to provide for his family disgruntled him. Twain had Elisha Bliss send Kitty Barstow all the books she wanted, guaranteeing the bill himself.[50]

Twain's scorn for William Barstow helps explain his next major decision. Seeking to establish a more permanent position before marriage, Twain borrowed $25,000 from Livy's father to purchase a one-third share of the Buffalo *Express*. He moved to Buffalo in August 1869 and began co-editing the paper. Twain's co-ownership of the *Express* represents an effort to provide for the family he was about to start, but it also reflects his impatience, paralleling his earlier acceptance of the secretaryship under William Stewart. In other words, he sought a stable position instead of waiting to see how his latest literary venture played out. In this instance he became an owner and editor of the *Express* before knowing how the public would receive *The Innocents Abroad*.

The book was a runaway success. *The Innocents Abroad* sold well, and the critical response was overwhelmingly positive. Many newspapers the *Express* received as exchanges reviewed *The Innocents Abroad*. One said Twain 'must henceforth be thought of first in connection with whatever is humorous in travel', comparing his humour with Thomas Hood's and finding not just humour but 'a deeper vein of sense and of feeling'.[51]

Twain's lecture tour that winter functioned as a book tour. Everywhere he went he witnessed the success of *The Innocents Abroad*. He informed Elisha Bliss, 'I never wander into any corner of the country but I find that an agent has been there before me, and many of that community have read the book.'[52] Its commercial success let Twain know he could make a comfortable living as a writer without the drudgery of newspaper work.

The positive reviews included one in the *Atlantic*. Passing through Boston on his lecture tour, Twain stopped by the magazine's office to meet its author, William Dean Howells. When they first met, Twain was wearing a custom-tailored sealskin coat constructed with the fur on the outside: a symbol of his fondness for startling onlookers.[53] The deep and abiding friendship between Howells and Twain began on that cold, coat-wearing day. With Joe Twichell and, later, Henry H. Rogers, Howells would become one of Twain's three closest friends in adulthood.

The London edition appeared in two separately issued volumes, *The Innocents Abroad* and *The New Pilgrim's Progress*. Both were generally well received. Thomas Hood enjoyed *The Innocents Abroad* but thought it lacked the 'screaming fun' of *The Celebrated Jumping Frog*. Sometimes the fun of *The Innocents Abroad* was lost on British readers. One London reviewer commented, 'It is not always easy to tell when the author is laughing and when he is serious.' *The Field*, the self-styled country gentleman's newspaper, offered a glowing review. The only aspect of the second volume *The Field* disliked was its title, suggesting instead 'The New Gulliver's Travels'.[54] *Innocents Abroad* would be translated into Danish, Dutch, German and Swedish over the next ten years. Speaking of the book's European reception, Joseph Conrad remembered, '*Innocents Abroad* was all the rage.'[55]

The book's success led to further writing opportunities. *Galaxy*, a New York monthly, invited Twain to contribute a regular column to its pages. The money was good; even better was the editorial freedom the magazine promised. Over the next year, Twain published numerous satirical pieces in the magazine, including 'The Late Benjamin Franklin', in which he depicts Franklin from a child's perspective. When children engaged in frivolous, unproductive behaviour, their parents would throw the example of Franklin in their faces: 'Nowadays a boy cannot follow out a single natural instinct without tumbling over some of those everlasting aphorisms and hearing from Franklin on the spot.'[56] Even as he critiques Franklin's famous sayings from *Poor Richard's Almanack*, Twain cannot deny their power. Decades later he would compile his own set of maxims for 'Pudd'nhead Wilson's Calendar', which he would use as chapter mottos for *Pudd'nhead Wilson*. Twain liked them so well he wrote 'Pudd'nhead Wilson's New Calendar' to use as chapter mottos in *Following the Equator*.

Twain ended this season's lecture tour in the third week of January – with good reason. He was getting married. The week

Langdon Clemens, 1871, photographic print.

before their wedding, Twain responded to a letter he had received from Jim Gillis. While announcing his marriage, Twain struck a melancholy note as he remembered the good times they had on Jackass Hill: 'It makes my heart ache yet to call to mind some of those days.'[57]

On 2 February 1870 in Elmira, New York, Samuel Clemens married Olivia Langdon. Twichell came from Hartford to assist. The day after the festivities, Jervis Langdon escorted the newlyweds to Buffalo, where he presented his wedding gift, a large, fully furnished, fully staffed house at 472 Delaware Street. Had Jervis Langdon understood his new son-in-law a little better, he might have waited before presenting such an extravagant gift. Twain was already questioning his future as a newspaperman and, thus, his future in Buffalo.

Jervis Langdon had little time to enjoy his new son-in-law. On 6 August 1870, at 61, he succumbed to stomach cancer. Three months later, on 7 November, Livy gave birth to a boy, whom they named Langdon. To announce the birth to Joe and Harmony Twichell, Twain wrote a letter in which he assumes the voice of his five-day-old son.[58] 'Langdon' tells the Twichells:

> They all say I look very old and venerable – and I am aware, myself, that I never smile. Life seems a serious thing, what I have seen of it . . . and my observation teaches me that it is made up mainly of hiccups, unnecessary washings, and wind in the bowels.

5

The River

After signing the contract for *The Innocents Abroad*, Mark Twain had anticipated spending a couple months in Hartford, Connecticut, working with Elisha Bliss to prepare the manuscript for publication. He informed his mother, 'I have to spend August and September in Hartford – which isn't San Francisco.'[1] Written less than two weeks after he first visited Hartford, this statement conveys a preference for San Francisco and thus contradicts a letter Twain wrote to the *Alta California*, in which he calls Hartford 'the best built and the handsomest town I have ever seen'. With feigned incredulity, he says that almost no one in Hartford drank, smoked, swore or chewed tobacco.[2]

Others have typically taken Twain's appreciation of Hartford in the *Alta* at face value.[3] The letter to his mother suggests his feelings were more ambivalent. Neither the public letter nor the private one should be read as expressions of his true feelings. In both cases Twain was toying with his readers. He idealized Hartford to unsettle Californians; he idealized San Francisco to tease his mother, much as he teased her by exaggerating the bad habits of good friends.

As he crested his thirties, Mark Twain, the man from the middle of the continent, found himself caught between either coast, between the rip-roaring good times of the West and the effete sophistication of the East, between where he had been and where he was headed. Joe Twichell helped him reconcile his mixed feelings for Hartford. An athlete and a preacher, Twichell spent his life – body and soul

– reconciling opposites. In 1871 Twain and his family left Buffalo to settle in Hartford.

Initially they rented a house in Nook Farm, a neighbourhood on the city's west side. Though Livy had inherited a quarter of a million dollars from her father's estate, Twain still wanted to support the family on what he could earn without exhausting her inheritance or, at least, without exhausting it too quickly. In October 1871 he left the family in Hartford to begin a fifteen-state lecture tour. In Bennington, Vermont, five weeks into the tour, Twain received the specimen copy for *Roughing It* and enjoyed the selections Elisha Bliss had made.

Confident *Roughing It* surpassed *The Innocents Abroad*, Twain knew it could succeed on its own merits but worried the market for books about the American West was so glutted there was scarcely room for one more. Already he was projecting a new book: 'the Mississippi book'. He planned to revisit the river for two months, take notes and create what he called 'a standard work'.[4] Over the next decade and a half, one prominent motif in Twain's writings would rise above the rest: the Mississippi.

During his lecture tour, some places reminded Twain that riverboat days were receding into the past. After lecturing in Steubenville – 'the best town site on the Ohio', according to old steamboat men – Twain spent the night at a local seminary. He reflected, 'These windows overlook the Ohio – once alive with steamboats and crowded with all manner of traffic; but now a deserted stream, victim of the railroads. Where be the pilots[?]'[5]

A three-week gap in his lecture schedule let Twain return to Hartford in February 1872 to celebrate both his wedding anniversary and his new book. His worries about the book proved unfounded. Readers loved *Roughing It*. Karl Kron, for one, enjoyed the way its author presented himself. A statement Twain makes in his preface – 'Information appears to stew out of me naturally' – gave Kron a model for presenting the material in his idiosyncratic cycling guide,

Ten Thousand Miles on a Bicycle. *Overland Monthly,* a San Francisco literary magazine, compared Twain with buffalo and grizzlies – two icons of the American West – observing, 'His genius is characterized by the breadth, and ruggedness, and audacity of the West.' And Henrietta Cosgrove called *Roughing It* 'the most thrilling realistic portrayal of frontier life ever given to the world'.[6]

Twain had another cause for celebration the following month. As a new baby neared, he and Livy went to Elmira to be near Dr Rachel Gleason, one of the first female physicians in the United States. With her husband Dr Silas Gleason, she operated the Elmira Water Cure, a hundred-bed sanatorium located partway down the hill from Quarry Farm, the rural property outside Elmira that Jarvis Langdon had given Susan after her marriage to Theodore Crane. The Gleasons advocated a common-sense medical approach that included walking, eating simple food and wearing loose-fitting clothes, but hydrotherapy formed the core of their medicine. Drinking it, bathing in it, swimming in it, the Gleasons' patients immersed themselves in water, a primeval, health-giving fluid that returned them to the element that represents the beginning of all earthly things and thus offered them a symbolic rebirth.

On Monday evening, 18 March, Livy showed signs that she would soon go into labour. The family sent word down the hill; Rachel Gleason came up the hill. She prepared everything upon her arrival and then slept at Quarry Farm to be ready in a flash. Twain kept watch as Livy rested. Around four that morning, he woke the doctor. Livy gave birth to a healthy baby girl an hour later. They named her Olivia Susan 'Susy' Clemens after her mother – a family tradition – and her aunt Susan Crane, who called the newborn 'a bright nice little creature [who] looks exactly like her Father'.[7]

Out of town seven weeks later, Twain wrote Susy a letter conveying what he felt and giving her a keepsake to read when she was older:

Susan Crane, undated, photographic print.

Many's the night I've lain awake till 2 o clock in the morning reading Dumas and drinking beer, listening for the slightest sound you might make, my daughter, and suffering as only a father can suffer, with anxiety for his child.[8]

Less than three months after Susy was born, her brother died. Having taken Langdon for a carriage ride on a cool morning, Twain, a glutton for guilt, blamed himself, though diphtheria, not exposure, caused the boy's death. Livy would subsequently give birth to two more daughters, Clara Langdon Clemens on 8 June 1874 and Jane Lampton 'Jean' Clemens on 25 July 1880.

In August 1872 Twain travelled to England for the first time. He wanted to advertise himself to English readers, find a British publisher for his future books to subvert the troublesome piracies and research a satirical book about England. He quickly realized he was already well known there as a humorist. Britain's literary community embraced him. Twain was so pleased with his visit he abandoned plans to satirize the nation: he liked England too well. He would return many times in the coming years.

Twain began *The Adventures of Tom Sawyer* in late 1872. He kept writing into the new year, as an impromptu weather report inscribed on the surviving manuscript demonstrates: 'Never forget the splendid jewellery that illuminated the trees on the morning of Jan. 9, '73. Brilliant sun and gentle, swaying wind – deep, crusted snow on ground – all the forest gorgeous with gems'.[9] Later that year he purchased a five-and-a-half-acre tract in Nook Farm on which to build a home for his family.

In late January Twain set *Tom Sawyer* aside to collaborate with Charles Dudley Warner, another Hartford neighbour, on *The Gilded Age*. Twain's contributions to the novel include a dramatic steamboat race that results in tragedy when a boiler explodes and causes numerous fatalities: a veiled retelling of his brother Henry's death. The most memorable character Twain created for *The Gilded Age*

Livy and the Girls (left to right: Susy, Jean, Livy, Clara), *c.* 1885, photographic print.

was Beriah Sellers. He later made the character the hero of *Colonel Sellers*, a lucrative and long-running play. Twain would often try to duplicate its success. Never again would he write a successful play.

Since his marriage, Twain and his growing family had begun to spend summers at the farm. For Twain, summers at Quarry Farm recalled summers at the Quarles farm. Southwestern New York was not dissimilar to the Old Southwest. The people who lived in the hidden hollers directly east of Elmira resembled the country folk directly west of the Mississippi. And Uncle Dan'l had a kindred spirit at Quarry Farm, too: Susan Crane's cook Mary Ann 'Auntie' Cord.

Auntie Cord loved to amuse the Clemens girls. 'She had ghosts and witches in stock' and filled their heads with legends that gave them nightmares. She shared her superstitions, too: 'The weather, the phases of the moon, uncanny noises, and certain eccentricities of insects, birds, cattle and other creatures all spoke to her in mystic

Quarry Farm exterior, *c*. 1900, photographic print.

Quarry Farm interior, *c.* 1890s, photographic print.

warnings.'[10] In Auntie Cord's kitchen Twain's daughters enjoyed experiences like those he had enjoyed himself in Uncle Dan'l's kitchen.

Her personal story inspired 'A True Story, Repeated Word for Word as I Heard It', the first article Twain contributed to *Atlantic*. Its subtitle is imprecise. Auntie Cord jumped back and forth in time as she told the story orally, but Twain kept it chronological. Otherwise 'A True Story' reflects her experience. Twain later included it in *Sketches, New and Old*. Inscribing a copy for Auntie Cord, he mentioned 'the bit of personal history which she recounted to him once'.[11]

Structured as a frame tale, 'A True Story' begins in Mark Twain's voice before 'Aunt Rachel' takes over. The story demonstrates Twain's distinctive ability to fuse Southwestern humour with other discursive genres: a dual impulse that defines his best work. In

'A True Story' he combines the frame-tale structure and interest in dialect common to Old Southwest humour with a sentimental story of motherhood.

Born into slavery, Aunt Rachel inherited her mother's catch phrase: 'I wa'n't bawn in de mash to be fool' by trash.'[12] Falling on hard times, her master sold her whole family, separating Aunt Rachel, her husband and all their children. Her son Henry eventually escaped to the North, where he became a barber and began searching for his mother. When the Civil War broke out, he joined the Union army but never abandoned his search. Though separated from her for thirteen years, he eventually found his mother working as a cook in North Carolina. Together her catchphrase and his boyhood scars let them recognize one another. Aunt Rachel, the story's inside narrator, re-enacts the recognition scene by physically placing Mark Twain in Henry's position. Mark Twain, the story's outside narrator, engages in a parallel form of doubling, serving as a stand-in for the reader. In her fine appreciation of 'A True Story' Lee Smith observes that Twain's tale forces us 'to open our minds and hearts as we listen'.[13]

Before the Clemens family reached Elmira in April 1874, Susan Crane – bless her heart – had a study built for her brother-in-law on a knoll at Quarry Farm. An octagonal building with windows all around, it offered a commanding view of the valley below. Describing his new study to Joe and Harmony Twichell, Twain exclaimed, 'When the storms sweep down the remote valley and the lightning flashes above the hills beyond, and the rain beats upon the roof over my head, imagine the luxury of it!'[14] The study proved an ideal place to write. Inside the octagon Mark Twain took on *Tom Sawyer*.

Ned Wakeman wrote to Twain that summer, asking if he would write up his adventures. Twain told him he did not need a writer, only a stenographer. His reply offers a good gloss on *Tom Sawyer*, emphasizing the importance of capturing the vernacular, of transferring the words of a great storyteller to the written page with as little editorial intrusion as possible:

> If your book has been taken down in short-hand, word for word as it fell from your lips, with your inaccuracies and peculiarities of speech unmarred, it *is a readable book* and needs no doctoring of mine. If some literary blacksmith has put it into fine language, no amount of doctoring can make a readable book of it.[15]

Mark Twain at the window of his study, 1903, photographic print.

Exterior view of Mark Twain's house, 351 Farmington Avenue, Hartford, Connecticut, undated, photographic print.

Twain added four hundred manuscript pages to *Tom Sawyer* before getting stuck in September. Though frustrated with his inability to finish the manuscript, he gradually understood his creative process while writing *Tom Sawyer*. To get unstuck he needed only to set the manuscript aside and work on other projects. Once he returned to *Tom Sawyer* months later he could pick up where he had left off:

> When the tank runs dry you've only to leave it alone and it will fill up again, in time, while you are asleep – also while you are at work at other things, and are quite unaware that this unconscious and profitable cerebration is going on. There was plenty of material now, and the book went on and finished itself without any trouble.[16]

Twain would continue to apply this creative process, which meant he often had several books in progress simultaneously. Some would take years to complete.

Late that September Twain and his family returned to Hartford and moved into 351 Farmington Avenue, their new Nook Farm mansion. Architecturally the house is bizarre. It has three turrets, five balconies and a wraparound veranda. The exterior is faced with dark brick, trimmed in brownstone and decorated with inlaid brick painted scarlet and black. The roof is covered with intricately arranged coloured tiles. The house has five bathrooms, all with indoor plumbing and, on Livy's instigation, custom-made porcelain washbasins decorated with designs to match the figures in the carpet.

Since the mansion remained unfinished when they first moved in, the family had to sleep in a guest room on the second floor while workmen completed the first. Twain had to deal with the architect, builder, carpetlayer, foreman, upholsterer, everyone who was involved in the home's construction. As if these workmen were insufficiently annoying, who should show up one day but a door-to-door book canvasser or, as Twain joked, 'a book *agent*, whose body is in the back yard and the coroner notified'.[17]

Twain always was a show-off: the new house manifests this longstanding impulse. Furthermore, he prided himself on being a good neighbour and a gracious host. Like his Nook Farm neighbours, he had an open-door policy. People were welcome to stop by and visit whenever they wished. Female visitors gathered in the parlour while Twain welcomed the men to the billiard room on the third floor. Practically every room contained something to amuse their guests.

The Clemenses' Hartford home, though fabulous, was not ideal. The luxurious house, combined with its daily visitors, required a large domestic staff and a vast outlay for upkeep and entertainment, which forced Twain to keep writing popular books to generate sufficient income to afford it. Just because Twain coined the term 'Gilded Age' does not mean he was immune to its excesses. He, too, fell victim to the materialism that defined the era. In the long run his need to surround himself with symbols of his success adversely affected his writing and ultimately sabotaged the natural talent responsible for his success in the first place.

Though the house demanded Twain write, it refused to let him write. Nowhere in his Nook Farm mansion could he concentrate on his work. From the mid-1870s and through the following decade – the most fruitful period of his career – Twain wrote his best stuff during the family's summer holidays at Quarry Farm within his octagonal study.

For his peace of mind, the nicest feature of their new home was its access to the footpaths that wove through the nearby woods. He and Twichell often went walking together, sometimes covering 10 miles for the purpose of 'enjoying a social chat and exchanging views on nothing in particular and everything in general'.[18]

Swayed by the current fad for pedestrianism, Twain and Twichell attempted a more ambitious walk in 1874. They planned to hike from Hartford to Boston, a hundred miles by the old stage road. Competitive pedestrians often did 'centuries', covering a hundred miles in 24 hours. Twain and Twichell allowed three days to go the distance. Livy supplied her husband with self-addressed envelopes to keep her posted. They left Hartford at 8:30 a.m. on Thursday, 12 November 1874. By 11 a.m. they had reached Vernon, Connecticut, where they stopped long enough for Twain to write to Livy. A tiny town, Vernon had few amenities. Most likely they stopped at George B. Thayer's grocery store. Twain's letter captures their joy:

The day is simply *gorgeous* – perfectly matchless. And the *talk!* Our jaws have wagged ceaselessly, and every now and then our laughter does wake up the old woods – for there is nothing to restrain it, there being nobody to hear it.[19]

An hour after dark they reached Grant's Hotel, having hiked 28 miles that day. That was the good news. The bad news? Twain's knees had begun to ache 3 or 4 miles back. They set out early the

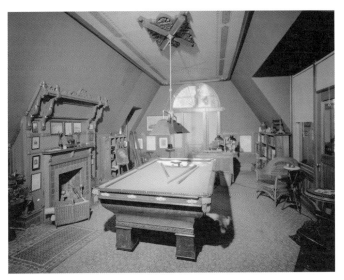

The billiard room of Mark Twain's house, undated, photographic print.

next morning, Friday the thirteenth. The woods were white with frost; Twain's knees were wracked with pain. After 6 miles they cut their walk short, stopping at a roadside tavern. The tavernkeeper agreed to drive them to the nearest railway station, where they could catch the next train, reaching Boston in time to attend a party that evening. When someone asked if they had walked from Hartford, Twain wryly commented that they had walked far enough to prove it could be done. The exercise had given him a fearsome appetite. Howells, the one who had invited them to the party, remembered Twain scarfing down scalloped oysters that evening.[20]

During another walk closer to home Twain told Twichell about his glory days as a Mississippi riverboat pilot. Fascinated, Twichell urged him to write up his recollections for the *Atlantic*. Twain pitched the idea to Howells, who also recognized its potential. Given their encouragement, Twain got to work. The result was 'Old Times on the Mississippi', a masterpiece in seven parts.

Like *Roughing It*, 'Old Times' is fictionalized autobiography. Both works reconstruct their author's personal past from years earlier, and each resembles a *Bildungsroman*. Like so many American literary classics, 'Old Times' is a story about a young man who refuses to follow in his father's footsteps and runs from home to find his way in the world. We readers can relate to the story Twain tells in 'Old Times'. His experiences resemble our own, regardless of profession. Reading how Twain learned to be a riverboat pilot, we remember how we learned our profession: how intimidating it was at first; how many mistakes we made; how we became overconfident as we learned, which only led us into further error; and how we mastered the profession only upon accepting the humility success requires.

Taken together, the articles that comprise 'Old Times on the Mississippi' amount to approximately 40,000 words, long enough for a short book but too short for a subscription book. Seeing that he could combine 'Old Times' with his projected work about the Mississippi, Twain avoided issuing 'Old Times' as a book. Others did not. Belford Brothers, a Toronto firm, pirated the magazine series and published it separately in 1876 as *Old Times on the Mississippi*. Ward, Lock & Taylor, a London firm, released it as *The Mississippi Pilot* in 1877. That same year George Robertson published the similarly titled Australian edition.

As a distinct work, *The Mississippi Pilot* has largely been forgotten, but in its day the book commanded a respectful following around the world. A Tasmanian reviewer found it Twain's best book so far, observing:

> Mark Twain has so enriched his *Pilot* with extraordinary facts, and spiced it with wit and quaint humor, as to make it not only the most amusing, but one of the most instructive little books of the day. No captain of a vessel, no mate, no seaman, no passenger afloat or ashore, and above all no river pilot in the world should be without Mark Twain's *Pilot*.[21]

Joseph Conrad was one seaman who would not be without *The Mississippi Pilot*. The London edition remained in print through the 1880s, when Conrad, then a young officer in the British merchant marine, picked up a copy at a London bookstall. Though it had 'a beastly glazed cover', Conrad did not judge *The Mississippi Pilot* by it. 'There was life inside it,' he said. Conrad vividly remembered how Twain learned to navigate the river: 'I thought of *The Mississippi Pilot* and of Twain while I was in command of a steamer in the Congo and stood straining in the night looking for snags. Very often I thought of him.'[22] In short, *The Mississippi Pilot* gave rise to *Heart of Darkness*.

Writing 'Old Times on the Mississippi', Twain sparked memories that helped him resume *Tom Sawyer*, which he had not touched for nine months. Between mid-May and early July 1875, he wrote another four hundred manuscript pages to complete the first draft. Upon learning Twain had finished the draft, Howells asked to see it. Despite his characteristic bluster and bravado, Twain was self-conscious about showing the manuscript to Howells. Before doing so, he made hundreds of revisions. Howells loved the work but thought Twain should publish *Tom Sawyer* as a boys' book, not as a book for grown-ups. Livy agreed. Twain accepted their opinion and followed the changes Howells recommended.[23]

Having completed the manuscript, Twain still had to arrange its publication. He wanted to issue the British edition first to protect *Tom Sawyer* from piracy. In June 1876 Chatto & Windus released *The Adventures of Tom Sawyer* to popular and critical acclaim. Newspapers around the globe published extracts illustrating the book's most iconic moments. The episode relating how Tom Sawyer got his fence whitewashed became an instant classic.[24]

Tom Sawyer appealed to people of all ages. The book made many reviewers feel like children again. The London *Examiner* was impressed with Twain's virtuosity. Aware of 'Jumping Frog' and *The Innocents Abroad*, the reviewer knew their author as both a humorist and travel writer. With *Tom Sawyer* he mastered the boys' book.

While understanding its appeal to youthful readers, the *Examiner* recognized much more: 'The book will no doubt be a great favourite with boys, for whom it must in good part have been intended; but next to boys we should say that it might be most prized by philosophers and poets.'[25]

An enthusiastic review appeared in the London *Morning Post*. Beyond its ability to recreate the milieu of childhood, *Tom Sawyer* also possesses antiquarian interest, the *Post* averred. Its reviewer read the folk beliefs and customs Twain recorded in *Tom Sawyer* with relief, happy to see that American materialism had not effaced Anglo-American folklore. *Tom Sawyer*, the *Post* continued, reinforced the cultural ties between the United Kingdom and the United States. The book's folklore

> shows how strongly the Anglo-Saxon strain must still affect those descendants of the ancient stock across the ocean, and how, in spite of materialism, the beliefs and superstitions of a race will abide and be handed down from father to son . . . Those boyish charms for the recovery of lost property, and the curing of warts, and what not; why they are the very incantations that have prevailed in Sussex and Warwickshire and elsewhere from time immemorial.[26]

Huckleberry Finn reinforced the importance of Twain's works as compendia of traditional customs and superstitions. A British reader called Twain 'one of the foremost of American *folkloristes*, though he generally preserves his traditions in his romances of *Tom Sawyer* and *Huckleberry Finn,* not in the proceedings of learned societies'. Contemporary readers recognized that Twain was not merely using folklore as local colour. He recorded traditional superstitions and customs to help assure their survival. Three years after *Huckleberry Finn,* its author became a founding member of the American Folklore Society.[27]

By placing *Tom Sawyer* with Chatto & Windus, Twain had circumvented British literary piracy, but Canadian publishers ignored imperial law and continued to pirate Twain's works. Shortly after the English edition reached Toronto, Belford Brothers released a pirated *Tom Sawyer*, which appeared in late July, months before the American edition would appear. The Toronto edition, which sold for as little as 75 cents, flooded the North American market, undercutting the u.s. edition, which would not appear for several months and then at a much higher price. When Harriet Wasson canvassed northern California, she discovered that many people had already read *Tom Sawyer*.[28]

Tom Sawyer presented another problem as a subscription book, which Wasson's experience verifies. Recruiting subscribers solely on the basis of the prospectus, she was shocked upon obtaining copies of *Tom Sawyer* to distribute. It was much shorter than the typical subscription book. Conveying her shock, Wasson said that the complete volume was scarcely longer than her specimen copy. She explained, 'The tantalizing gaps of the prospectus were connected only by a very short literary thread.' She feared her subscribers would refuse the book. Only one refused, but, she said, 'Everybody was disappointed by the smallness of their books.'[29]

In its first year *Tom Sawyer* sold poorly, compared to *The Innocents Abroad* or *Roughing It*. Those two works each sold over 60,000 copies their first year. *Tom Sawyer* sold fewer than 24,000 copies. His modern editors explain: 'From Mark Twain's point of view the early sales of *Tom Sawyer* were deeply disappointing, even disastrous.'[30]

From the viewpoint of almost any other author, sales of nearly 24,000 copies in a single year would be cause for celebration. The same year Twain published *Tom Sawyer* Herman Melville published *Clarel*, a long and challenging narrative poem. *Clarel* sold barely a hundred copies in its first three years, after which the publishers pulped the unsold copies.[31] By the time he reached *Clarel* Melville had decided to write whatever he wished regardless what the public

E. W. Kemble,
Huckleberry Finn,
frontispiece engraving
from Mark Twain,
*Adventures of
Huckleberry Finn
(Tom Sawyer's
Comrade)* (1885).

thought. He refused to compromise his art for the sake of sales.
Twain, alternatively, not only wanted to make a living as a writer,
but wanted to live extravagantly on the proceeds of his pen. He
continually adjusted his writing to suit his readers, admitting:
'My books are water; those of the great geniuses are wine.
Everybody drinks water.'[32]

Even before Twain finished *Tom Sawyer*, he had begun planning
its sequel. He wanted to write it as a first-person narrative but knew
Tom did not have the breadth and depth of character – the moral
gumption – to tell the story. Huck Finn did. Spending the summer
of 1876 at Quarry Farm, Twain finished reading the page proofs
for *Tom Sawyer* and took on a new challenge: *Huckleberry Finn*.

Huck famously begins: 'You don't know about me, without you have read a book by the name of *The Adventures of Tom Sawyer*, but that ain't no matter.' Huck's first sentence has a conversational tone that puts readers at ease. As Wallace Martin observes, his dialect and poor grammar effectively authenticate the narrative.[33] Huck's words involve the reader in the task of interpretation, showing that his identity depends on their perception. He defines himself in negative terms. Instead of stating who he is, Huck acknowledges their ignorance of him.

Though Huck makes no explicit comment about his identity in the opening, his diction reveals much. In American English, few words are more telling than 'ain't'. Huck's use of this vulgarism brands him as uneducated and lower-class. The rest of the sentence, however, forms a counterpoint to this impression. Curious about how he has been portrayed, Huck himself has read *Tom Sawyer*. Unwilling to let that book stand as the record of his life, Huck has enough savvy to create his own self-portrait for the reading public. Instead of letting readers form an impression of him based on what Mark Twain says in *Tom Sawyer*, Huck prefers to tell his own story.[34]

The introduction also forms an innovative experiment with the frame-tale structure. *Adventures of Huckleberry Finn* is not technically a frame tale, but, by having Huck make reference to *Tom Sawyer*, Twain attaches *Huck Finn* to the earlier book, essentially turning it into the opening frame for the later one. More than a clever marketing device (though it is that too), Twain's narrative strategy in *Huckleberry Finn* presents a groundbreaking variation in the Old Southwest tradition. The strength of Huck's narration obviates the need for an outside narrator beyond the brief reference to *Tom Sawyer*.

After introducing himself, Huck describes life with the Widow Douglas. Before the opening chapter closes, he mentions sneaking out one night to join Tom Sawyer's new band of robbers. Before the third chapter ends, Huck has matured beyond Tom's shenanigans, though he has yet to realize it. When Huck subsequently fakes his own death to escape his abusive father and later when he and Jim are on the raft together, Huck wishes Tom Sawyer were around, prompting readers to think, 'No, you don't.'

That summer Twain took Huck as far as the Grangerford farm, that is, partway into Chapter Eighteen. What he wrote so far did not yet include a three-chapter block relating the wreck of the *Walter Scott* but did include Chapter Sixteen, which contained the celebrated raftsmen episode. This, one of the finest episodes he wrote for *Huckleberry Finn*, relates how Huck and Jim approach a big raft filled with men who make their living and live their lives on the river. Jim decides Huck should swim to the raft and learn more about their precise location. Once aboard, Huck finds a good hiding spot and listens to the boastful and boisterous conversation.[35] He soon hears the Child of Calamity, a version of the ring-tailed roarer, a character type vital to the American folk tradition:

Whoo-oop! I'm the old original iron-jawed, brass-mounted, copper-bellied corpse-maker from the wilds of Arkansaw! – Look at me! I'm the man they call Sudden Death and General Desolation! Sired by a hurricane, dam'd by an earthqua!:e, half-brother to the cholera, nearly related to the small-pox on the mother's side! Look at me! I take nineteen alligators and a bar'l of whisky for breakfast when I'm in robust health, and a bushel of rattlesnakes and a dead body when I'm ailing! I split the everlasting rocks with my glance, and I squench the thunder when I speak! Whoo-oop! Stand back and give me room according to my strength! Blood's my natural drink, and the wails of the dying is music to my ear! Cast your eye on me, gentlemen! – and lay low and hold your breath, for I'm 'bout to turn myself loose!

As Huck listens to the men, he learns about a mysterious barrel that has haunted the river for years, making a sound resembling a baby's cry. It supposedly contains the body of an infant named Charles William Albright. After one raftsman wonders how it could cry for so long, another responds, 'Well, never mind how it could cry – how could it *keep* all that time?' Soon after the story is told, the raftsmen discover Huck and ask his name, whereupon he replies, 'Charles William Albright, sir.'[36]

His reply reinforces the theme of Huck as a changeling. Earlier he had been caught trying to pass himself off as a girl. Assuming Albright's identity, Huck assumes the role of a wild child. Whereas the legendary wild child is raised by wolves, Huck depicts himself as a boy who had been abandoned to the river in his infancy and now emerges from it thirteen years later. He has been raised by the river. When a raftsman catches his fib, Huck is unfazed. He drops the Albright identity and instantly takes up another. Huck has learned to improvise and rapidly invents a back story for himself.

In the section of *Huckleberry Finn* Twain wrote during the summer of 1876, Huck shows considerable maturity. Though he has a natural-born moral sense, Huck is the product of his environment – the antebellum South – and must unlearn what society has taught him before he can fully develop. The rattlesnake episode provides one opportunity for moral growth. While Huck and Jim hide out together on Jackson's Island, Jim gets bitten by a rattlesnake because Huck had tried to play a trick on him. Jim attributes the bite to having handled an old snakeskin, which, like looking over the left shoulder at a new moon, could bring bad luck. Jim's superstition reflects something Twain had heard from Auntie Cord, who believed 'the discoverer of a sloughed snake-skin lying in the road was in for all kinds of calamities'.[37]

Huck closes the rattlesnake episode with an anecdote about a man who had looked over his shoulder at the moon:

Old Hank Bunker done it once, and bragged about it; and in less than two years he got drunk and fell off of the shot tower and spread himself out so that he was just a kind of a layer, as you may say; and they slid him edgeways between two barn doors for a coffin, and buried him so, so they say, but I didn't see it. Pap told me. But anyway, it all come of looking at the moon that way, like a fool.[38]

Huck's humour is dark; his motivation is murky. By changing the subject from the rattlesnake to the new moon, he deflects attention from his culpability in Jim's snakebite, essentially refusing to own up to it. Not until Huck plays another prank on Jim further down the river does he acknowledge the impropriety of such practical jokes. The extent of Huck's gullibility also seems uncertain. He cites Pap as his source. Did Pap dupe Huck, who took what he said as gospel, or did Huck recognize that Pap had told a stretcher? If Huck did recognize his father's hyperbole, then the son has become like his father, at least when it comes to telling tales. Repeating this tall tale, Huck attempts to dupe us, his readers, as Pap had attempted to dupe him.

Once the raft is run over by a steamboat, he and Jim get separated, and Huck ends up at the Grangerford farm. Unsure where to take the story next, Twain set *Huckleberry Finn* aside, as he had earlier set aside his partially completed *Tom Sawyer* manuscript, to wait until he was ready to resume the story. He would not return to *Huckleberry Finn* until 1880.

Twain kept busy during the intervening four years. Seeing himself as both an inventor and an entrepreneur, he always had one scheme or another in the works. Most failed, but one invention turned a profit: a self-pasting scrapbook. Since Dan Slote was still manufacturing blank books, Twain approached him with the idea. Slote saw merit in it. To avoid sticky fingers and protect treasured mementos, Twain envisioned a scrapbook patterned on the self-sealing envelope. Each page would contain two gummed areas that needed only be moistened to prepare them to hold whatever scraps the collector wished to save. Starting in 1877, Slote published *Mark Twain's Patent Self-pasting Scrap Book* at different price points in different formats, some designed for photographs, others for newspaper clippings.

Slote also agreed to publish *Punch, Brothers, Punch! and Other Sketches,* a collection of Twain's recent magazine fiction. The collection did not sell well, but it did attract some appreciative readers. Identifying it as 'one of Mark Twain's funny books', a San Francisco reviewer found *Punch, Brothers, Punch!* 'a cure for the dyspepsia'. The collection promoted the scrapbook, which was advertised at the back. Some booksellers used *Punch, Brothers, Punch!* as a premium, giving it away to anyone who purchased a high-end scrapbook.[39]

After setting *Huckleberry Finn* aside, Twain went to Bermuda with Twichell. He chronicled their trip as 'Some Rambling Notes of an Idle Excursion', a four-part series for the *Atlantic.* 'Hurricane' Jones, a loud-talking sea captain tattooed from head to heel who sailed the Pacific for over half a century, is the most memorable character of 'Some Rambling Notes'. Based on Ned Wakeman, who had recently passed away, 'Hurricane' Jones let Twain commemorate his friend. Karl Kron found something else to admire about 'Some Rambling Notes'. Twain's thousand-word description of the roads in Bermuda was so precise that Kron reprinted it in *Ten Thousand Miles on a Bicycle.*[40]

Further travels gave Twain the subject for his next book, *A Tramp Abroad*. In April 1878 he and his family took a trip to Europe, which extended into August 1879. Though he had signed a contract for *A Tramp Abroad* beforehand, Twain struggled with it. He wrote from Europe, inviting Twichell to join them. Twain hoped his friend's presence would inspire him. Twichell accepted the invitation and came to Europe, but even the reverend could not save *A Tramp Abroad*. Though a commercial success, *A Tramp Abroad* is a critical failure. It has a few bright moments. A. E. Housman called the ascent of Rigi-Kulm 'the most deliciously humorous thing in the whole of Mark Twain', and Karl Kron liked the Swiss bedbugs, which Twain calls the legendary wild chamois.[41]

'Jim Baker's Blue Jay Yarn' – the book's third chapter – is generally considered its best. This fable, which Twain first heard Jim Gillis tell back on Jackass Hill, is delightful when read in itself, but it poorly suits *A Tramp Abroad*. Coming so early in the book, 'Jim Baker's Blue Jay Yarn' forms a long digression in another voice before Twain establishes the book's narrative footing. It reads like a *mise en abyme*, replicating *A Tramp Abroad* in miniature. Accidentally dropping an acorn down a hole in the roof of a cabin, a blue jay decides to fill the hole with acorns, unaware he has an entire cabin to fill. The other birds get a good laugh upon learning what Blue is doing. With *A Tramp Abroad*, Twain attempts to fill the vast space of a six-hundred-page subscription book with anecdotes. No matter how many acornesque anecdotes he adds, the narrative still seems empty.

The best bits of humour Twain acquired in Europe never made it into *A Tramp Abroad.* An aficionado of bawdy jokes, he recorded the 'snappers' of many he heard during the trip in his travel notebook. Though he loved retelling these racy jokes orally, his burgeoning sense of decorum prevented him from putting them into *A Tramp Abroad.*

One snapper he recorded mentions an ailing patient whose small stature made medical diagnosis difficult.[42] Though Twain never put this joke into print, J. W. Sherman, a Maine physician, did. A few years later Dr Sherman embedded the joke within an otherwise serious essay he contributed to the *Massachusetts Medical Journal*. In a masterful instance of telling a joke with a straight face, Dr Sherman relates several well-documented instances of misdiagnosis before explaining:

> I can conceive of circumstances where the diagnosis might be involved in some doubt – as when once a lady applied to

a physician for advice, she being so short of stature, the doctor was unable to determine whether she had an ulcerated sore throat or piles.[43]

Twain did find at least one way to share his bawdy jokes in Europe. In spring 1879 he was invited to present a speech in Paris at a dinner hosted by the Stomach Club, a group of men who loved ribaldry. Twain presented 'Some Thoughts on the Science of Onanism', a speech containing many fanciful quotations supporting onanism from such famous figures as Homer, Julius Caesar and Franklin. He also cited some contemporary figures, including Cetshwayo kaMpande, the Zulu king who, according to Twain, once said, 'A jerk in the hand is worth two in the bush.' Twain summarized his own views on onanism: 'As an amusement it is too fleeting; as an occupation it is too wearing; as a public exhibition there is no money in it.'[44]

Finishing *A Tramp Abroad* in early 1880, Twain returned to *Huckleberry Finn* by mid-March. He extricated Huck from the Grangerfords, but not without a gun battle so gory Huck cannot bear to recount its details. Twain reunited Jim and Huck and got them back on the river, to their relief – and ours. Huck presents their conversation in indirect discourse. He and Jim now almost speak as one: 'We said there warn't no home like a raft, after all. Other places do seem so cramped up and smothery, but a raft don't. You feel mighty free and easy and comfortable on a raft.'[45]

The river welcomes Huck and Jim with open arms, protecting them with its embrace, providing comfort and companionship while serving as a place of refuge. Both lifeblood and lifeline, the river rescues and sustains them, saving Huck and Jim from the danger and duplicity of the land, where neighbour fights neighbour, where one man can own another, where greed and hypocrisy rule. The river washes away all the deception and connivery, leaving those who surrender to it in peaceful bliss.

The calm does not last, however. Twain continued the story through Chapter 21, that is, long enough to introduce two of the biggest scoundrels in American literature, the King and the Duke. Twain set the manuscript aside in May, intending to return to it at Quarry Farm, but he spent the summer of 1880 writing *The Prince and the Pauper*. He would not resume *Huckleberry Finn* until 1883.

The Prince and the Pauper is Twain's sell-out book. Choosing a reactionary genre – the historical romance – and appealing to a genteel audience, Twain wrote the book that middlebrow, middle-class East Coast readers wanted him to write. He buried the Mark Twain voice he had spent years cultivating and wrote the book in an impersonal style. In one place, and one place only, does he reflect the Mark Twain of *Tom Sawyer* and 'Old Times on the Mississippi'. Describing how Tom Canty – the pauper who switches places with the prince – adjusts himself to the English court, the third-person narrator explains, 'Time wore on pleasantly, and likewise smoothly, on the whole. Snags and sandbars grew less and less frequent.'[46] In sixteenth-century London, where the book is set, the Thames was an open sewer: that wasn't sand on the river bottom. Twain, for a brief moment, let his impersonal style slip to reveal the persona of the nineteenth-century Mississippi boatman.

Published in December 1881, *The Prince and the Pauper* met with enthusiastic praise, which seems astonishing in retrospect. Many reviewers found it Twain's best book yet. Though it represents his concession to Eastern readers, Western readers enjoyed it, too. The *Sacramento Daily Union* observed, 'It is so very different from anything that he has before attempted, that it comes as a most agreeable surprise.'[47] Joe Goodman dissented. He wrote to Twain to express his disappointment with *The Prince and the Pauper*: 'It might have been written by anybody else – by a far less masterly hand, in fact. You went entirely out of your sphere.'[48]

Twain finally returned to the Mississippi in 1882, accompanied by James R. Osgood, his new publisher. Throughout the preceding decade Twain had been growing increasingly frustrated with the American Publishing Company. After Elisha Bliss died in 1880, Twain signed with Osgood, whose list included some of New England's most prestigious authors. Osgood proved to be a congenial companion during their trip down the Mississippi, but he lacked both the experience and the infrastructure Twain needed to continue successfully publishing his books by subscription.

The 1882 river journey gave Twain sufficient material to finish *Life on the Mississippi* and resume *Huckleberry Finn*. By late May 1882 he had a plan to assemble his disparate materials for *Life on the Mississippi*. The first two chapters would supply some historical background regarding the river's exploration. He would borrow the raftsmen episode from *Huckleberry Finn* for Chapter Three. Its inclusion would not only supply some excellent local colour, but would provide advance publicity for *Huckleberry Finn*. Twain would use the raftsmen episode in the specimen copy for *Life on the Mississippi,* as well. For chapters Four to Seventeen he would reuse 'Old Times on the Mississippi', splitting the seven periodical instalments into fourteen chapters. Chapters Eighteen and Nineteen would retell his brother Henry's death. The rest of the book would relate his 1882 journey, heavily padded with historical source material.

Life on the Mississippi was well received, though reviewers almost unanimously agreed that its first half, the part containing the raftsmen episode and 'Old Times', was far superior to the second.[49] Neither *Life on the Mississippi* nor *The Prince and the Pauper*, the two subscription books Twain published with Osgood, sold as well as those he had published with the American Publishing Company. Always quick to blame others for his own shortcomings, Twain blamed Osgood for the poor sales. It did not occur to Twain that the weakness of the book's second half may have adversely affected sales. He attributed its commercial failure to Osgood's specimen copy, which, except for the raftsmen episode, largely consisted of chapters derived from 'Old Times', a work now a decade old. People who recognized the material would not want to subscribe to a book that recirculated so much previously published text.

As *Huckleberry Finn* neared completion, Twain had to decide how to publish it. Committed to subscription publishing, he broke with Osgood. He considered returning to American Publishing, now operated by Elisha's son Frank Bliss, but ultimately formed his own publishing company, making his nephew-in-law and business manager Charles Webster nominal head. The firm was called Charles L. Webster & Co., but make no mistake: Mark Twain pulled the strings.

Corresponding with Webster, Twain stressed the importance of the canvassing process. Once *Life on the Mississippi* was set in type, Twain restored the raftsmen episode to *Huckleberry Finn* but told Webster to omit it from the specimen copy. He did not want to repeat what Osgood had done with *Life on the Mississippi* and include previously published text in the specimen copy.[50] Though omitting the raftsman episode from the prospectus, he fully intended to include it in *Huckleberry Finn*.

Planning how to market the book, Webster and Twain considered partnering with American Publishing to promote *Tom Sawyer* and *Huckleberry Finn* together. Though it was the sequel to *Tom Sawyer*, *Huckleberry Finn* was a much bigger book, not just in terms of scope but in sheer number of pages. To make it more closely resemble *Tom Sawyer*, the new book would need some cutting. Citing Howells as his authority, Webster suggested they cut the raftsmen episode from *Huckleberry Finn*. Sometimes Twain was a poor judge of his own writing. He acquiesced to Webster's suggestion without a fight, ignoring how instrumental the raftsmen episode is to Huck's development.

American Publishing subsequently refused to cooperate, so the two books would not be marketed together, thus obviating the need to trim *Huckleberry Finn*. By the time marketing plans were settled, the book's production was too far along to restore the episode, so *Huckleberry Finn* appeared without it.[51] Twain's keenest readers have regretted its absence. Writing in the early twentieth century, British essayist E. V. Lucas hoped the next edition of *Huckleberry Finn* would appear with the raftsmen episode 'in its true place'.[52] The episode would remain absent until Twain's modern editors restored it while preparing the standard edition of *Huckleberry Finn* for the book's centenary.

Chatto & Windus published the London edition of *Adventures of Huckleberry Finn* in December 1884, with the u.s. edition appearing early the following year. The book sold well, making Twain's first venture as a publisher a success. Readers generally saw the book as a contribution to the literature of American humour. One London reviewer enjoyed the atmosphere of the Mississippi valley, which seemed so different from England, observing, 'There is never a moment's cessation of fun of a peculiarly fresh, bright kind, not to be found in our land of fog and east wind.'[53] Though many praised *Huckleberry Finn*, contemporary reviewers failed to see the book's greatness. Recognition of it as a masterpiece of American literature would await the twentieth century.

6

The Wheel and the Wire

Once he finished drafting *Adventures of Huckleberry Finn*,
Mark Twain gave himself a treat: he bought a bicycle. To suit
his competitive nature, he acquired a Columbia Expert with
a 50-inch wheel, the same model the best long-distance cyclists
rode. By late April 1884 Joe Twichell had also obtained a high-
wheeled bicycle, and the two men learned to ride together.[1] They
were in good company. Hartford, the home of Columbia bicycles,
had a lively cycling culture. Many wealthy neighbours rode bicycles
and even formed their own cycling club, the Asylum Hill Club.
Florine Thayer McCray, who lived a stone's throw from Mark
Twain's mansion, wrote *Wheels and Whims*, the earliest cycling
novel in American literature.[2] Most high-wheeled cyclists were
younger men. Twain, who had turned 48 in November, was a little
old to take up cycling. So was Twichell, at nearly 46, but the lure of
the bicycle, a method of exercise and transportation that combined
man and machine, was undeniable.

Twichell's decision to start riding a bike was not without
controversy. Some parishioners found it an undignified form
of transportation inappropriate for men of the cloth. Pedalling
preachers aggressively defended their right to bike. Beyond its
health benefits, two-wheeled travel was more economical than
four-hoofed travel. Though bicycles were still fairly expensive
– a Columbia Expert cost about a quarter of a factory worker's
annual salary – they were still cheaper than keeping a horse.

Changing religious attitudes helped clergymen justify strenuous physical exercise. Protestant leaders feared Christianity was becoming too effeminate. Christ had been reduced to a meek, mild figure. It was time to remake his image, to show that Christ had the strength of a chucker-out who could toss moneychangers from the temple and the endurance of an outdoorsman whose campcraft helped him survive a forty-day wilderness experience. Muscular Christianity encouraged parishioners and clergymen alike to participate in athletics.[3]

When Twain took up cycling he hired an instructor from the Columbia factory, a young German who was 'a gentle, kindly patient creature, with a pathetically grave face'. The instructor always put Twain back on his bike after he fell off. By all accounts, he fell off quite often. At one point his instructor told him, 'Mr Clemens, you can fall off a bicycle in more different ways than any person I ever saw before.'[4]

By the third week of the month, references to their newfound activity were appearing in the press. A nationwide celebrity, Twain made good copy. On 18 May 1884 the *St Louis Globe-Democrat* announced, 'Mark Twain has become a convert to bicycling.'[5] Later that week Twain informed Ned House:

> There *is* a live issue here . . . It is this: whether Twichell and
> I will beat the bicycle, or whether the bicycle will beat us.
> We have fought the creature a couple of weeks, now, and
> we have honorable wounds to show for it. This morning we
> traveled a couple of miles, mainly up hill, – and made it derned
> uncomfortable for the wagons; for *they* could never tell just
> which way we were proposing to steer – and neither could we.[6]

A story that circulated in the press depicts Twain and Twichell riding together side by side. Since this anecdote survives in multiple versions with varying details, it sounds more like folklore than fact.

After Twain took a header, the story goes, Twichell slowed to help his friend. Twain supposedly said, 'Don't stop, Joe; go right along. I think I'll stop here a while to swear.'[7]

Twain's two-wheeled efforts inspired 'Taming the Bicycle'. With H. G. Wells's *Wheels of Chance* (1896) and Jerome K. Jerome's *Three Men on the Bummel* (1900) – both cyclotouring novels – Twain's essay ranks among the top three funniest works about bicycling in the English language. It contains much self-effacing humour depicting Twain's wobbly attempts to ride a bike. Dismounting from a high-wheeler, for example, was especially difficult. Twain observes, 'Try as you may, you don't get down as you would from a horse, you get down as you would from a house afire. You make a spectacle of yourself every time.'[8]

Adding to the fun, Twain included a smart-aleck boy to comment on his troubles. One time after Twain falls, the boy suggests he ride a tricycle instead. The boy's suggestion emasculates Twain. Though trikes had a devoted following in Great Britain, in the United States they were ridden mainly by women. The boy essentially tells Twain to ride a girl's bike. Overall 'Taming the Bicycle' is a delight, the two-sentence closing paragraph especially so: 'Get a bicycle. You will not regret it, if you live.'[9]

Twain intended to publish 'Taming the Bicycle' in the New York *Sun* and had sent the manuscript to Charles Webster to prepare it for publication. In the first week of June 1884 Twain had second thoughts. He wrote Webster: 'I revised, and doctored, and worked at the bicycle article, but it was no use, I didn't like it *at all* – so I tore it up.'[10] He then requested that Webster tear up the manuscript in his possession. Happily, Webster ignored Twain's request. Two versions of 'Taming the Bicycle' survive. An unpublished version survives in manuscript among Webster's papers at Vassar College. A later version, which Webster had typed, was not published in Twain's lifetime but Albert Bigelow Paine, his literary executor, included it in the 1917 collection *What is Man? and Other Essays*.[11]

The numerous differences between the two versions confirm both the time Twain spent on 'Taming the Bicycle' and his uncertainty regarding the work. In the published version Twain depicts himself as a total buffoon as he tries to ride. In the earlier version Twain demonstrates his cycling prowess. His dissatisfaction with the essay suggests his indecision regarding which tone he wished to convey.

A previously unrecorded newspaper report hints that the essay came closer to publication in 1884 than Twain admitted. Besides preparing the essay for publication, Webster apparently prepared a press release announcing it. The newspaper report shows an insider's knowledge of the essay's contents – and gives away its ending: 'Mark Twain is tackling the bicycle, and the country may shortly expect a humorous exaggeration on the difficulties and trials of the inexperienced wheelman – if Mark lives.'[12]

The newspaper notices caught the attention of Richard Garvey, whom Twain had met in Rome years earlier. Now living in St Louis, Garvey was president of the Missouri Bicycle Club and an officer of the Missouri Wheel Company. He welcomed Twain as a brother wheelman and sent him one of his company's products, a Duryea saddle. Garvey asked Twain to test the saddle, and, if he liked it, to write an endorsement. Garvey was not the only businessman who sought a product endorsement from him. The previous year Mark Twain had registered his name as a trademark, and, in the coming years, he would rent his face out for cigar boxes, tobacco premiums and cigarette coupons.[13]

The Duryea saddle combined lightweight and easy adjustability to make a more comfortable saddle than those that came on Columbia bicycles.[14] Twain apparently agreed to test it out. Onto Garvey's letter, he wrote, 'Sho', meaning, 'Sure'. If he did start using the saddle, he did not keep using it. Twain's bicycle survives at the Connecticut Historical Society, but its saddle is not a Duryea.

In July, over two months after he began riding, Twain left Hartford for his annual Quarry Farm sojourn. He informed a correspondent,

'I've brought a bicycle here to this mountain-top, and if you will wait a while, *that* can be made to furnish you some [news].'[15] Having his bike with him at Quarry Farm, Twain revealed the confidence he had in his cycling abilities. He did little riding that summer, however. The road from Elmira up Watercure Hill to the farmhouse, which ascends nearly 650 vertical feet in the last mile – an average gradient of over 10 per cent – was far too steep to ride his 50-inch Columbia. Writing to Twichell from Quarry Farm towards the end of the summer, Twain admitted that he had tried to ride once at Quarry Farm but took a hard fall. He explained, 'There is no chance here for the art – the hills are long and steep, and one would have to walk back after riding down.'[16] Twain's letter shows that he never actually rode down Watercure Hill Road. The descent on a high-wheeler would require the temperament and athleticism of a daredevil.

Concluding the unpublished version of 'Taming the Bicycle', Twain asserts that he did master how to coast, an acrobatic manoeuvre that involved throwing the legs over the handlebars:

> It was a cold day, so to speak, that I took a chance at 'coasting', I mean, putting your legs up over the tiller and letting the machine go flying down hill like a racer. I had seen others do it, and as it was the only ordinary feature of bicycling which I had not tried I thought I would sample it. I chose a good enough hill, except that it was too steep. It was very fine, and breezy, and exhilarating sport till I got half way down; then I noticed – for I have a sharp ear – that I was keeping exactly abreast the middle words of a telephonic message concerning a sick child which were traveling along a wire above my head, and this furnished me with the sudden and frightful conviction that I was going perilously fast; so without an instant's thought, I put a mighty grip on the brake; and of course was flung thirty feet into the air. But I did not regret it. I struck that wire, and got the closing words about

the child – it was better, thank heaven, it was better. I had been uneasy about the child.[17]

With these dynamic words, Twain links two forms of modern technology, the bicycle and the telephone. They share a common theme: speed. Trains were faster than bicycles, of course, but the train was not personal transport. Before the invention of the automobile, the bicycle provided automobility. In other words, the bicycle was the first type of transport to emphasize the relationship between technology and personal mobility.[18] The telephone gave consumers a similar autonomy. To send a telegram, a person had to visit a telegraph office and have an operator send the message. Those who received telegrams were also beholden to not-always-reliable telegraph boys to deliver them. Both the bicycle and the telephone empowered individuals, freeing them from dependence on others.

As the unpublished version of 'Taming the Bicycle' suggests, Twain's interest in the telephone parallels his interest in the bicycle. In 1877, the year after Alexander Graham Bell patented the telephone, Isaac D. Smith, the proprietor of the Capitol Avenue Drug Store in Hartford, strung a telephone line between his store and a doctor's office in town. By year's end, seventeen others had subscribed to the service. Most subscribers were physicians, but they also included the Hartford *Courant*, a few local businesses and one private residence: the Clemens home on Farmington Avenue.[19]

Twain's correspondence shows that he recognized the telephone's potential for nationwide communication. Before telephone lines linked cities together, he saw how to combine telephone and telegraph to communicate with people across the nation. He could telephone the *Courant* office and dictate a telegram to the operator, who could then send it wherever telegraph wires reached. The communication process also worked in the opposite direction. The *Courant* office could receive telegrams for Twain, ring him up and read their contents to him over the telephone, thus eliminating flighty telegraph boys altogether and accelerating the communication process.[20] Imagining a way to combine telegraph and telephone, Twain sensed the possibilities of modern communication technology. Though he would grumble about the telephone sometimes, its possibilities continued to fascinate him. He subsequently obtained a teleharmonium, an electromagnetic device for transmitting music via telephone lines.[21]

As the telephone extended its reach, Twain boasted about his early recognition of its powers. Speaking with one interviewer, he identified himself as the first man in New England to put a telephone in his home, but, he continued, 'it was constantly getting me into trouble because of the things I said carelessly.'[22] Twain understood the dangers of rapid communication. Letter writing let people carefully consider what they said and avoid snap judgements, but the telephone made it all too easy for someone to speak without sufficient consideration.

Twain was also the first to use the telephone in fiction. The same year he had a telephone installed in his home, he wrote a short story in which the phone figures prominently, 'The Loves of Alonzo Fitz Clarence and Rosannah Ethelton'. Though this burlesque of sentimental courtship fiction is seldom discussed among Twain's best work, its importance grows the longer the telephone endures.

The story begins on a raw and gusty day in Eastport, Maine. Trapped indoors by the snow, Alonzo 'Lon' Fitz Clarence is so bored he hardly knows what to do. Too lazy to go downstairs to check the time, Lon telephones Aunt Susan to ask her. She lives in a different time zone, so he must convert her time to local Maine time: still easier than walking downstairs. This early in the story, and in the telephone's history, Twain saw how the new invention fostered laziness and thus undermined its autonomy. Giving people the opportunity to contact others for information, the telephone lets them avoid thinking for themselves.

Temporarily withholding Aunt Susan's precise location, Twain indicates her distance from her Down East nephew by saying she lives where it is 'warm and rainy and melancholy'.[23] The mystery provokes our curiosity, which Twain ultimately satisfies by revealing that she lives in San Francisco. Speaking with his aunt, Lon overhears a young woman singing 'In the Sweet By and By', an old-fashioned ditty that was a favourite target of Twain's satire. Over the telephone Aunt Susan introduces Lon to Rosannah Ethelton, and the two speak at length. After saying goodbye to Rosannah, Lon exclaims to himself, 'Two little hours ago I was a free man, and now my heart's in San Francisco!' Beyond what it means to the story, Lon's exclamation holds biographical significance. Though Twain had put down roots in Hartford, he never stopped longing for San Francisco.

Lon and Rosannah continue to telephone one another, and they also exchange photographs, another technology that intrigued Twain, the most photographed nineteenth-century author in American literature. When Sidney Algernon Burley, Rosannah's former beau, overhears one of their telephone conversations, he plots revenge. Sidney travels across the continent to Maine, where he passes himself off as a preacher-turned-inventor to sell Lon a device to prevent anyone from wiretapping the phone and listening to his lovey-dovey conversations with Rosannah.

When Lon briefly leaves the room, Sidney takes advantage of his absence and speaks on the telephone with Rosannah. Pretending to be Lon, he criticizes her old-fashioned singing. He offends her so much she splits up with Lon. After considerable time and effort, though still without meeting face to face, Lon and Rosannah clarify their differences. They wed over the telephone and take separate honeymoons. Sidney gets his comeuppance, and Lon and Rosannah finally meet.

'The Loves of Alonzo Fitz Clarence and Rosannah Ethelton' demonstrates how modern communication technology can alter interpersonal relationships. Sidney's behaviour reveals how easy it is for someone to assume a false identity over the telephone. Lon and Rosannah show how a man and a woman living thousands of miles apart can fall in love without meeting. Twain's prescience is extraordinary. Writing barely a year after the telephone's invention, he anticipates twenty-first-century social media.

Twain's fascination with modern technology would reach its zenith in *A Connecticut Yankee in King Arthur's Court*, a work that manifests both the nineteenth century's fascination with all things Arthurian and its belief in technological progress. Lord Tennyson's *Idylls of the King* triggered the Arthurian revival, and his principal source, Thomas Malory's *Morte d'Arthur,* received renewed attention. In 1880 Twain obtained Sidney Lanier's version of Malory, *The Boy's King Arthur*. Three years later he mentioned to a correspondent two leading characters from the story that would each figure in *Connecticut Yankee*, Sir Kay and Sir Launcelot. Twain gradually recognized that he could take a scion of modern industrial, technological America back to King Arthur's England with hilarious results.[24]

Instead of throwing himself into *Connecticut Yankee* after completing *Huckleberry Finn*, Twain devoted his time to Charles L. Webster & Co. Though he had established the firm to publish his own books, he soon had an opportunity he could not resist. After Ulysses S. Grant began contributing articles about the Civil War to *Century*, Twain approached him and offered to publish his memoirs by subscription. They signed a contract in February 1885, and Twain oversaw the book's production and promotion closely.

The general died shortly after completing the *Personal Memoirs of U. S. Grant*, which proved to be a masterpiece of military autobiography. Twain said it had only one equal: Caesar's *Commentaries*.[25] The first volume appeared in December 1885, the second in March 1886. It was a phenomenal success, earning Grant's widow over $400,000 in royalties – a record sum – and convincing Twain of his powers as a publisher.

Ulysses S. Grant, 1880, photographic print.

Twain would describe his friendship with Grant and the publication of *Personal Memoirs* at length in a section of his own autobiography. Titled 'The Grant Dictations', the section fills over thirty closely printed pages. These 'excruciating passages of hero worship of General Grant', Garrison Keillor has observed, remind readers that, as a writer, Grant could do something Twain could not: write a classic autobiography.[26]

With the success of Grant's *Personal Memoirs* Twain expanded the list of publications offered by Charles L. Webster & Co. He sought to duplicate the success of Grant's book, issuing other military memoirs and celebrity autobiographies – to little avail. One unusual title that stands out is King David Kalakaua's *Legends and Myths of Hawaii*. Twain's ongoing support for folklore studies partly explains his motivation for publishing Kalakaua's *Legends and Myths of Hawaii* – the first major work in English on the subject – but his acceptance of the book was personally motivated. Rollin

M. Daggett, Twain's old Nevada friend and, more recently, U.S. Minister to Hawaii, had befriended King Kalakaua and subsequently edited the book for publication. Twain's publication was a favour for an old friend, but it also provided personal vindication. Previously unable to publish an illustrated edition of his own Hawaii book, Twain demonstrated through his lavishly illustrated *Legends and Myths of Hawaii* that those publishers who had rejected his book had been wrong after all.

None of the books Twain published in 1887 or 1888 approached the success of Grant's *Personal Memoirs.* Kalakaua's *Legends*, for one, barely recouped its manufacturing costs.[27] Twain's inability to publish another best-seller, combined with his unwise investments and extravagant lifestyle, meant that he had an acute need for ready cash. By the summer of 1888, he returned to *Connecticut Yankee* convinced that the best way to publish a best-seller would be to write one himself.

The Paige compositor represents Twain's most foolhardy investment. In 1880 he had encountered James W. Paige, the inventor of an automatic typesetting machine. Unlike the competing linotype machine invented by Ottmar Mergenthaler, the Paige compositor was based on the human analogy. In other words, it mechanically mimicked the process of setting type manually. It was like a human, only better. Twain used to joke that the machine 'could do all things a human typesetter could do, and do them faster and better, except talk, eat, drink, smoke and go on a strike'.[28] Ever since apprenticing as a printer, Twain had continued to take an interest in printing technology. The opportunity to make a revolutionary contribution to its development and a vast fortune for himself he found irresistible.

Paige – 'the Shakespeare of mechanical invention', Twain called him – was also a smooth talker.[29] He had to be to secure the investment necessary to pursue his inventions. Twain fell for Paige's spiel. Through the 1880s he poured a fortune into the impossibly complex machine. His letters that decade testify to his grand dreams of great wealth derived from this newfangled compositor. They read like the letters he wrote during his silver-prospecting days. In both instances, the fortune Twain foresaw always seemed close but was never within reach.

Though Paige constructed his first working model in 1887, it required further modifications and additional investment. Confident of its eventual success, Twain poured the profits from Charles L. Webster & Co. into Paige's invention. Having depleted the company's coffers, Twain hoped *Connecticut Yankee* would provide a sizeable influx of cash. When he and his family went to Quarry Farm in 1888, he worked on the manuscript throughout the summer but had not finished it before they returned to Hartford. Determined to keep working, he took over an upstairs room in Joe Twichell's house to avoid the continual distractions at his own home.[30]

Before Twain finished *Connecticut Yankee*, Charles L. Webster & Co. underwent a major change. In February 1888 Frederick J. Hall replaced Webster as manager. Hall had been with the firm since the mid-1880s. He had helped prepare Grant's *Personal Memoirs* for publication and, in 1886, had become a partner. At the end of 1888, Webster retired altogether, and Fred Hall bought out his interest in the firm.

Writing *Connecticut Yankee*, Twain saw a symbiotic connection between the book and the Paige compositor, then under construction across town at the Pratt and Whitney machine shop. In the first week of October 1888 Twain expressed hope that he would finish the book around the same time Paige finished the compositor.[31] Both *Connecticut Yankee* and Twain's manic investment in the compositor exemplify his ambivalence towards technology. Obsessed with the wonders of technology, he nevertheless recognized its dangers, its ability to control behaviour, to enslave people, to make them minions of the machine.

Daniel C. Beard, *Sir Boss*, engraving from Mark Twain, *A Connecticut Yankee in King Arthur's Court* (1890), p. 69.

Connecticut Yankee begins in Mark Twain's voice as he tours Warwick Castle, where he meets a stranger, who visits him at his hotel that evening and starts relating his personal story. The stranger is Hank Morgan, the Connecticut Yankee himself, who says he was mysteriously transported back to sixth-century England. Hank gives Twain a manuscript in which he relates what had happened. Once Hank nods off, Twain begins reading his narrative.

Twain's frame-tale structure in *Connecticut Yankee* shows him continuing to experiment with elements of Old Southwestern humour. Though a Hartford native, Hank echoes earlier inside narrators in the same tradition. Relating how he introduced newspaper editing and printing to medieval England, Hank says he trained Clarence, his protégé, as a journalist. Clarence's journalistic style soon reaches 'the back-settlement Alabama mark, and couldn't be told from the editorial output of that region either by matter or flavor'. Later encountering a newspaper filled with printing errors, Hank remarks, 'It was good Arkansas journalism, but this was not Arkansas.'[32]

Though Hank is a Connecticut native, his humorous treatment of Alabama literacy and Arkansas printing does not necessarily reflect the viewpoint of a Northerner looking down his nose at barely literate Southerners. Rather, Hank's comments represent another tradition of Southern humour, the willingness to make fun of those from another state, an impulse that helps citizens define the individual character of their own state. In American culture, paradoxically, interstate antagonism can strengthen regional and national unity.[33]

Both the setting and the situation of *Connecticut Yankee* represent further variants of the Old Southwest tradition. Typically, a stranger would visit a Southern locale, have difficulty adapting or understanding what he sees and assume a superior attitude only to become the object of humorous derision. In *Connecticut Yankee* Hank is the stranger in a strange land, yet he is the one who gains the advantage over the natives. Having Hank travel in time, not space, Twain further advances his prose, fusing a prominent motif of science fiction with the traditions of the Old Southwest.

Hank Morgan introduces all sorts of modern technology to King Arthur's medieval world. He has men run telegraph and telephone lines throughout England but hopes to keep the new communication network low-key: 'They were stringing ground wires; we were afraid to put up poles, for they would attract too much inquiry.'[34] Hank understands that making technology too obvious would make it too intimidating.

Once set in motion the new technology almost propagates itself. Astonished to come across a hermit's den converted into a telephone office one day, Hank takes comfort in what he sees and hears:

> It sounded good! In this atmosphere of telephone and lightning communication with distant regions, I was breathing the breath of life again after long suffocation. I realized then, what a creepy, dull, inanimate horror this land had been to me all these years, and how I had been in such a stifled condition of mind as to have grown used to it almost beyond the power to notice it.[35]

Not everything Hank says about the telephone is positive. He gets riled by 'noise', to use the term Claude Shannon, the founder of information theory, coined to identify the fundamental problem with the telephone. When a message is encoded into a signal, transmitted across a communication channel to a receiver, decoded and handed to its destination, it can be affected by noise, that is, anything that distorts, deforms or otherwise affects the signal during the transmission process.[36] When Hank identifies his location – 'Valley of Holiness' – over the telephone, the person on the other end of the line mishears it as the 'Valley of Hellishness'. Hank's frustration with noise is palpable: 'Confound a telephone, anyway. It is the very demon for conveying similarities of sound that are miracles of divergence from similarity of sense.'[37]

Later in the book, while Hank and King Arthur tour the kingdom incognito, they are captured and sold into slavery.

Hank escapes and heads to the nearest telegraph office to contact Clarence and have him send Sir Launcelot with a squadron of five hundred knights to rescue the king. Meanwhile, Hank's escape angers the slavemaster so much that he whips the other slaves, who rise up and kill him. Consequently, all the slaves are condemned to hang the next day.

When Hank is recaptured, he boasts that no one will hang, whereupon their captors change the execution date from tomorrow to today. Hank estimates that the knights will arrive three hours too late to rescue them. Just as their captors prepare to stretch the king's neck, who should appear but 'five hundred mailed and belted knights on bicycles', which Hank finds 'The grandest sight that ever was seen. Lord, how the plumes streamed, how the sun flamed and flashed from the endless procession of webby wheels!'[38]

The notice of *Connecticut Yankee* in *The Wheel and Cycling Trade Review* quotes this last sentence, recognizing a possible source for Twain's image of several hundred knights cycling together: 'Mark must have got his idea from the general meet in the park, so you see that much-abused gathering has secured cycling a big advertisement.'[39] During the 1880s many cities across the United States held bicycle meets attracting hundreds of riders. Hartford, Connecticut, for one, hosted an annual tournament starting in 1884. Though some citizens objected to hundreds of cyclists parading through their streets, people generally witnessed these parades with awe and enthusiasm.[40]

The Wheel and Cycling Trade Review continues, 'The fun of introducing all the latest triumphs of science amongst the people of Arthur's time is, in Mark Twain's hands, some thing immense.'[41] Much as Twain in real life combined two forms of technology – telephone and telegraph – to create an efficient communication network, in *Connecticut Yankee* he combines two forms of technology – telegraph and bicycle – to create a swift military response. The combination of modern transportation technology and modern communication technology – the wheel and the wire – lets Sir Launcelot win the day.

Dan Beard, the artist Twain hired to illustrate *Connecticut Yankee*, depicted Sir Launcelot atop a high-wheeler, but Twain's description in *Connecticut Yankee* is more flexible. Never does he specify what type of bike the knights ride. The year *Connecticut Yankee* appeared, 1889, was a turning point in cycling history. When the safety bicycle with two same-sized wheels appeared earlier that decade, serious cyclists scorned it. Not until 1889 did the safety bicycle achieve a degree of acceptance within the cycling community. Describing that year's Hartford tournament, George B. Thayer, now a freelance reporter, noticed that around half the bicycles in the parade were safeties.[42] Before long, Mark Twain himself would obtain a safety. As he learned to ride it, he had his daughter Jean run alongside to help keep him vertical. He questioned the name 'safety', calling his new bike 'the cussedest thing to tame I ever saw – twice as difficult as the old high wheel'.[43]

Sir Launcelot's rescue of the king in *Connecticut Yankee* represents the happiest use of technology in this technology-laden book, but it does require some qualifications. The preference for the telegraph over the telephone suggests that the most advanced technology is not necessarily the best. The telephone had a greater potential for noise to enter the system and obscure the message. Furthermore, telephone wires could be tapped and strategic military messages intercepted. Telegraph wires could also be tapped, but telegrams could be sent encoded with a cipher, a practice military commanders developed during the Civil War, as Twain knew from Grant's *Personal Memoirs*.

The bicycle, like the telegraph, is an intermediate form of technology. Though not invented until after the railway, it represents a simpler technology. While recognizing the combined usefulness of the telegraph and the bicycle in effecting the king's rescue, Hank never learns the dangers of too much technology. Once they return

Daniel C. Beard, *Launcelot Swept In*, engraving from Mark Twain, *A Connecticut Yankee in King Arthur's Court* (1890), p. 485.

to Camelot, he makes further technological advances. He soon has steamboats on the Thames, steam warships at sea and a railway connecting Camelot with London. When Hank goes to France on holiday, the Church puts England under an interdict, bringing his improvements to a halt. Most of his followers take the Church's side, leaving only himself, Clarence and 52 trained boys to make their stand at Merlin's cave.

Equipped with Gatling guns and other modern weapons to withstand the siege, they have also installed a weapon of mass destruction: a surrounding electric fence capable of electrocuting anyone who approaches. When they switch on the current, the fence slaughters 25,000 knights almost instantly. Hank and the boys would seem to be victorious, but they realize too late that they are trapped, surrounded by 25,000 rotting corpses.

In early November 1889, around the time Twain finished *Connecticut Yankee*, he read Edward Bellamy's *Looking Backward*, first published the previous year.[44] *Looking Backward* is the finest among many utopian and dystopian novels to appear during the late nineteenth century. *Connecticut Yankee* fits into the utopian literary tradition – at least in terms of form. For the most part *Connecticut Yankee* resembles a utopian novel by depicting a place where various technological improvements work together to improve people's lives, though its satirical tone undercuts the value of the supposed improvements. The utopia reaches its peak as the bike-riding knights, having been summoned by the telegraph, arrive in time to save Hank and the king. At this moment Twain created a utopia where technology and humanity have achieved an ideal balance. But the author knows what his hero does not: too much technology can be disastrous. In Hank's world technology takes control with devastating consequences. Unchecked technology ends in a dystopian nightmare.

7

Journey to the End of the Night

Telling William Dean Howells about *A Connecticut Yankee in King Arthur's Court* shortly before the book appeared, Mark Twain said, 'It's my swan-song, my retirement from literature permanently.'[1] Still anticipating the success of the Paige compositor, Twain looked forward to becoming a multimillionaire and foresaw the day he could stop writing for publication. No longer would he have to rely on his pen to afford his family's lavish lifestyle. His statement to Howells did not mean he would stop writing altogether. Never would he stop writing. It was part of him, part of his mind and his make-up. Writing functioned as a form of therapy for Twain, who wrote to vent his spleen, massage his ego and soothe his soul.

Though he would keep writing for the next two decades, *Connecticut Yankee* remains, in many ways, his swansong to literature. A step down from *Huckleberry Finn* in terms of creative achievement, *Connecticut Yankee* is nonetheless a major work in the history of American literature, a historical romance that captures the zeitgeist of the times in which it was written. Nothing Twain wrote afterwards would approach the ingenuity or the virtuosity he demonstrates in *Connecticut Yankee*.

The book was also a commercial success, but its income did not come close to rescuing its author from his investment in the Paige compositor, into which he would ultimately sink – the estimates vary widely – somewhere between $170,000 and $300,000.[2] Nor could *Connecticut Yankee* offset losses stemming from the unsuccessful titles Charles L. Webster & Co. had published. To prop up his personal investment in the compositor, Twain invited some of his best friends to invest. Joe Goodman, for one, agreed to invest in it. Goodman also tried to form a consortium of investors within the community of Nevada silver barons, but nothing came of his efforts.[3]

Unable to afford their extravagant life in Hartford, Twain moved his family to Europe to economize in June 1891, that is, once Susy left college after her freshman year at Bryn Mawr. Twain had had mixed feelings about his oldest daughter attending college. Though proud of Susy, he resented her growing independence. She seemed to be pulling away from him. During her freshman year, Bryn Mawr invited him to speak. Susy made her father promise not to tell 'The Golden Arm'. Apparently she considered the startle story too cornball for her sophisticated classmates. Oblivious of his daughter's feelings, Twain broke his promise and told 'The Golden Arm' anyway. Before he could yell, 'You've got it!', Susy had run from the auditorium in tears.

Once the family left for Europe, Fred Hall could manage Charles L. Webster & Co. without Twain looking over his shoulder. Hall faced an almost impossible task as he tried to save the business from ruin. The subscription publishing system on which the company had been based was becoming obsolete. In the 1890s it was limited more and more to multivolume sets issued on the instalment plan. *The Library of American Literature*, the multivolume set Charles L. Webster published, sapped whatever capital Paige did not take. Hall would phase out subscription publishing and turn the firm into a trade publisher.[4]

While his family lived in Europe, Twain often returned to America to oversee his business interests. He consulted with Hall during the trips home, but his principal focus remained the Paige compositor. To generate as much additional income as possible, Twain cranked out short stories, essays and travel sketches as fast as possible. The highest paid magazinist of the era, he could contribute to *Harper's* or the *Atlantic* whenever he wished. After publishing a spate of magazine articles, he would assemble them into a book-length collection and rush it into print.

Over the next three years Twain published several books. In 1892 he released a new novel, *The American Claimant*, for which he brought back the character of Colonel Sellers: a sign he was struggling to imagine any new characters; either that or he found it safer and more expedient to recirculate old characters than create new ones. *The American Claimant* is generally considered Twain's worst novel. That same year he published *Merry Tales*, an ironically titled collection that included 'The Private History of a Campaign that Failed'. *The £1,000,000 Bank-note and Other New Stories*, a collection of largely forgettable works of short fiction, appeared the following year.

In 1894 Twain published *Tom Sawyer Abroad*. The previous decade he had attempted to capitalize on his most beloved characters with 'Huck Finn and Tom Sawyer among the Indians' but abandoned the work after nine chapters. Now strapped for cash, he brought Tom, Huck and Jim back again in a blatant commercial effort to take advantage of their popularity. Like the other books he published in the early 1890s, *Tom Sawyer Abroad* failed to produce sufficient income to get Twain out of debt or let him bring his family home.

Instead of further collections, Twain needed a new novel, that is, a book with greater earning potential, a surefire hit he could throw together quickly. He devised an outrageous farce, *Those Extraordinary Twins*, which would take Angelo and Luigi Capello, a set of Siamese twins with one pair of legs and two torsos, and place them in situations that would let the humour flow. The number of possible comedic situations was almost limitless. Twain could dash off one episode after another until his manuscript reached book length. Conceiving *Those Extraordinary Twins* as a subscription book and composing it in Europe, Twain appears out of touch with the

Mark Twain's Pudd'nhead Wilson Dramatized by Frank Mayo, 1895, lithograph.

realities of the American book market, unaware that the method of publishing on which he had built his career was becoming passé.

A strange thing happened as Twain expanded *Those Extraordinary Twins*: the more he wrote the less farcical it became. The work began taking on serious undertones. Instead of the episodic structure he initially conceived, a plot – a murder mystery plot, no less – emerged. The twins declined in importance, and Twain reduced them to a subordinate role. Local attorney David 'Pudd'nhead' Wilson, originally a minor character, assumed a much greater role in revision, so great, in fact, that Twain made him the focus of the book and changed its title to *Pudd'nhead Wilson*. The character's fascination with fingerprints would let him solve the mystery. *Pudd'nhead Wilson* is the first novel to identify a murderer using fingerprint evidence.

In February Twain wrote to Hall to inform him that he had completed *Pudd'nhead Wilson* and had it typed but admitted that he was unsure what to do next. He considered sending it to the American Publishing Company, now being run by Elisha Bliss's son Frank, but Livy thought it would be inappropriate to let any other publishing house but their own issue *Pudd'nhead Wilson*. Twain refused to release it as a trade book: 'A book in the trade is a book thrown away, as far as money-profit goes.'[5]

Though he had a typescript of *Pudd'nhead Wilson* prepared, Twain revised the work further. He extracted some of the Angelo and Luigi sections from the text. Instead of completely eliminating the twins from *Pudd'nhead Wilson*, he kept them in but separated Angelo and Luigi from one another. No longer are they Siamese twins, just regular twins. Since the humour stemmed from their conjoined nature, the twin-related jokes in *Pudd'nhead Wilson* are not funny any more. Twain could have removed them altogether, but that would have been too much work: he couldn't be bothered.

Twain told Hall that after excising the conjoined twins from *Pudd'nhead Wilson* the resulting manuscript had a sharp focus:

The whole story is centred on the murder and the trial; from the first chapter the movement is straight ahead without divergence or side-play to the murder and the trial; everything that is done or said or that happens is a preparation for those events.[6]

Three characters, he continued, and three characters only – Wilson, Tom Driscoll and Roxana – stand out from the rest. Twain's assertion reflects wishful thinking. In truth, he had reworked the manuscript so quickly and carelessly that he left its text filled with ambiguities, anomalies and uncertainties.[7] What remains after he finished his 'literary Caesarean operation' is often confusing and difficult to follow. Richard Aldington found *Pudd'nhead Wilson* 'so unreadable that only the sternest sense of duty can compel a perusal'.[8]

Pudd'nhead Wilson is a chronicle of wasted opportunity. The most important work Twain had written since *Connecticut Yankee*, it embodies several major themes: slavery, miscegenation, prejudice, nature versus nurture, the value of forensic evidence. For *Pudd'nhead Wilson* he created some of his strongest characters since Huck and Jim. Roxana or 'Roxy', for one, is a spunky and outspoken woman who claims descent from 'old Cap'n John Smith, de highes' blood dat Ole Virginny ever turned out'.[9] A majestic mother-figure reminiscent of Auntie Cord, Roxy never hesitates to speak her mind but willingly sacrifices herself for her son's sake. Twain failed to recognize that he had something really special on his hands. Revising *Pudd'nhead Wilson,* he did not take the time to get it right, to develop his promising ideas and characters into a truly great novel. Instead he slapped the book together as quickly as he could, aiming for maximum profits with minimal effort.

During a visit to New York in September 1893, Twain arranged to serialize *Pudd'nhead Wilson*. It appeared in *Century* in seven monthly instalments from December 1893 to June 1894. Though he had hoped Charles L. Webster & Co. would publish the work, the firm declared bankruptcy in April, despite Hall's best efforts to keep it afloat. Twain returned to the American Publishing Company. *Pudd'nhead Wilson* was too short to make a subscription book by itself, so Twain took the text he had removed that summer, revised it slightly, retitled it 'Those Extraordinary Twins', wrote a tongue-in-cheek introduction and appended it to the main work, releasing the book as *The Tragedy of Pudd'nhead Wilson and the Comedy Those Extraordinary Twins*.

While Twain was in New York arranging for the serialization of *Pudd'nhead Wilson*, he befriended Henry H. Rogers. Their friendship would prove vital to Twain's financial well-being. A vice president of Standard Oil, Rogers had established a reputation as one of the most talented yet ruthless men on Wall Street. Overall, his business style had earned him the nickname 'Hell Hound'. His financial success let him amass a personal fortune of over $100 million. Though uncompromising in his business affairs, Rogers was quite genial in person, a warm and generous spirit with a wide circle of friends.

Once he and Twain became friends, Rogers offered to help him resolve his business problems. When Charles L. Webster & Co. declared bankruptcy, Rogers safeguarded Twain's assets. He assigned his copyrights to Livy. He also declared Livy the company's primary creditor – with good reason. Twain had been borrowing from his wife's estate all along. In addition, Rogers arranged a plan that would let Twain pay his debts.

Rogers also brought to an end Twain's investment in the Paige compositor. He initially saw value in the machine and invested some of his own money but soon became disenchanted. In October 1894 Paige arranged a trial run for his compositor at the *Chicago Herald*. It failed miserably. Present to witness the trial, Rogers concluded that the Paige compositor had no commercial value whatsoever and convinced Twain once and for all to abandon his hopes for the machine, cut all ties with Paige and accept his investment as a total loss.

In May 1895 Rogers helped Twain negotiate a contract with one of the nation's leading publishers, Harper & Brothers. The following year Harper would publish *Joan of Arc*. This historical novel has biographical significance: its eponymous heroine reflects Susy Clemens's personality. As literature, it is scarcely worth mentioning. George Orwell called it 'a namby-pamby "life" of Joan of Arc'.[10] Harper would also reissue *Tom Sawyer Abroad* with several short tales and another work that recirculated Twain's best-loved characters. All the individual works in *Tom Sawyer Abroad: Tom Sawyer, Detective and Other Stories* had been previously collected, except 'Tom Sawyer, Detective', which had recently appeared in *Harper's*. Taking advantage of the vogue for detective fiction stimulated by Arthur Conan Doyle's Sherlock Holmes, Twain made Tom and Huck detectives. 'Tom Sawyer, Detective' reflects Twain's declining creative powers. Turning Huck Finn into a Dr Watson, Twain diminished what he had achieved in *Huckleberry Finn*.

When Rogers arranged for Twain to pay off his debts, he negotiated a deal to pay his creditors pennies on the dollar. To Livy, ever Twain's moral compass, the deal seemed unethical. She insisted they pay off the entire amount dollar for dollar. Twain accepted her opinion, though he knew what it would entail. He would have to return to the lecture circuit. Instead of a transcontinental zigzag, his new lecture tour would take the form of a round-the-world extravaganza. Besides providing the income to pay his debts in full, it would also provide material for a new book of travels, *Following the Equator*.

Susy and Jean would stay with Aunt Susan at Quarry Farm, while Clara accompanied their parents on the lecture tour. They set out in mid-July. Twain delivered his first lecture in Cleveland to an enthusiastic audience. 'Mark Twain at Home', as he titled his new lecture, varied from night to night but generally included time-tested favourites: 'The Celebrated Jumping Frog of Calaveras County', 'The Golden Arm', 'Jim Baker's Blue Jay Yarn' and selections

Edward Penfield, *Harper's August*, 1896, lithograph. Penfield, art editor for *Harper's*, created some of the magazine's most striking and memorable covers. The cover of the August 1896 issue is typical, fresh and forward-thinking with bold outlines and primary colours that capture the zeitgeist of a new generation. In contrast, 'Tom Sawyer, Detective', which began in this issue, seems old-fashioned.

James B. Pond, *Mark Twain's North American Lecture Tour: Aboard the North Land*, photographic print, 1895. In this picture, taken aboard the *North Land* as it steamed across Lake Erie on the first leg of the round-the-world lecture tour, Livy berates Sam, telling him to put on a coat so he won't catch a cold.

from *Huckleberry Finn*. In Cleveland they boarded the *North Land*, a steamer that took them through Lake Erie and Lake Huron. After lecturing in Sault Ste Marie, Mackinaw and Petoskey, they steamed across Lake Superior to Duluth. From Minnesota they went to Winnipeg before returning to the u.s. to cut across Montana and Washington. The North American segment of the tour ended in British Columbia.

Twain hoped to visit San Francisco, but a detour there proved unfeasible. They sailed from British Columbia to Hawaii. A quarantine prevented them from landing at Honolulu, so they continued to Sydney, where Twain kicked off the Australian portion of his journey. He stuck with the 'Mark Twain at Home' theme, which suited Australia well, not only because he had an enduring Australian popularity that stretched back to *The Celebrated Jumping Frog of Calaveras County*, but because he felt at home among the Australian people. In *Following the Equator* he observes:

> The Australians did not seem to me to differ noticeably from Americans, either in dress, carriage, ways, pronunciation, inflections, or general appearance. There were fleeting and subtle suggestions of their English origin, but these were not pronounced enough, as a rule, to catch one's attention. The people have easy and cordial manners from the beginning – from the moment that the introduction is completed. This is American. To put it in another way, it is English friendliness with the English shyness and self-consciousness left out.[11]

Newspaper reporters interviewed Twain in nearly every Australian city he visited. Typically Livy and Clara stuck around during the interviews and sometimes supplied comments of their own. Speaking with the reporter for the Melbourne *Herald Standard*, Twain mentioned a kookaburra he had encountered in New South Wales.[12] Since Twain knew about the bird's characteristic laughter, this kookaburra took him aback. 'It sat on a tree, and I stood looking at it,' he explained. 'But it wouldn't laugh for me. I tried to make it laugh; indeed I did; but it respectfully declined.'

'Probably it didn't think you were funny,' Livy quipped.

Among the thousands of pages of published biographical material about Mark Twain and his family, perhaps no single sentence reveals more about Livy than the quip she made in

Melbourne. Twain's tendency to protect Livy, to place her on a pedestal, to elevate her above all the grime and muck that sullies the world, has largely prevented history from seeing her personality. All too often she seems two-dimensional, more type than person, the stereotypical Victorian woman, the kind of woman on whose head and in whose hands John Ruskin placed a myrtle crown and a stainless sceptre.[13] Livy's Melbourne quip offers a different view. It reveals her personality, her depth and her sense of humour, which happened to be a deadpan sense of humour she shared with her mother-in-law.

After a tour of other cities in the Melbourne area, Twain went to Tasmania and from there to New Zealand, where he spent most of November and half of December 1895 lecturing throughout the South and North Islands before resuming his Australian tour. On New Year's Day they left Adelaide for Ceylon and India. Twain found Bombay 'a bewitching place, a bewildering place, an enchanting place – the Arabian Nights come again!'[14] He lectured his way across India before making additional stops in Mauritius and South Africa. In mid-July they left Cape Town en route to Southampton, England, which they reached on 31 July 1896.

Susy and Jean were supposed to sail from America to meet the family in England. While visiting Hartford, Susy became seriously ill. Her condition was diagnosed as spinal meningitis. Livy and Clara quickly left England to nurse Susy, but they were too late. Susy, only 24, died on 18 August while they were en route. Alone in England Twain received the tragic telegram.

Following the Equator appeared in 1897. Chatto & Windus titled the British edition *More Tramps Abroad* to take advantage of the commercial success of *A Tramp Abroad*. Despite its connection to the earlier book, *Following the Equator,* as travel literature, represents a substantial improvement over *A Tramp Abroad*. It is a much more unified work. Sailing through the British Empire, Twain rode the wave of the Great Rapprochement, the time when Britain and the

United States formed the deep and abiding political, cultural and diplomatic relationship that endures to the present. The Great Rapprochement gives *Following the Equator* its continuity. Throughout the narrative Twain celebrates English-speaking people around the globe. Paradoxically, *Following the Equator* also manifests the anti-imperial rhetoric that would become a significant part of Twain's polemical writings over the ensuing decade.

These two unifying themes come together in Twain's description of Wanganui, New Zealand, where he viewed a monument to those who fell during the Maori wars. According to its inscription, the monument was erected in honour of the white men 'who fell in defence of law and order against fanaticism and barbarism'. Though Twain identified with the English who settled New Zealand, he objected to the inscription, which unnecessarily demeans the Maori. They were not fanatics, Twain observed. The Maori were patriots:

> They fought for their homes, they fought for their country; they bravely fought and bravely fell; and it would take nothing from the honor of the brave Englishmen who lie under the monument, but *add* to it, to say that they died in defense of English laws and English homes against men worthy of the sacrifice – the Maori patriots.[15]

During the summer of 1897 Twain and his family settled in Vienna, where Clara could pursue her singing career. The Austrians lionized Twain, and he moved in Vienna's most prestigious social circles. Notably, he also found time to write. He drafted 'The Chronicle of Young Satan', a work that would become *No. 44, The Mysterious Stranger*, a posthumously published historical fantasy set in fifteenth-century Austria. The different permutations of Twain's story all involve Satan, or a character like him, who enters a village, encounters several local youths and demonstrates the helpless futility of the human race and all it cherishes. Reading the *Mysterious Stranger* manuscripts, Louis Rubin found them consistent with much of Twain's later writings:

> They do not essentially alter the portrait of an aging writer whose final years were laced with gloom, depression, and despair, and who toiled away at unoriginal pessimistic denunciations of God and the human race which he could neither finish nor publish. Unfortunately, the 'Mysterious Stranger' material is not really very interesting; the cleverness palls after a few pages, and one soon tires of Twain's spinning out his interminable demonstrations of the wretchedness of man and the universe.[16]

The Clemenses visited many cities and met many people during their time in Europe. Jean's frail health – she had recently been diagnosed with epilepsy – brought the family to Sweden to attend Henrik Kellgren's summer institute. Dr Kellgren practised a form of osteopathy that emphasized massage and physical therapy. After two and a half months of treatment, Jean seemed to improve. When the family returned to England in October, they found lodgings near Kellgren's London institute, where she could continue her therapy.

Before another year passed, Twain decided to return to the United States, now convinced Jean could be treated in America as well as anywhere. One of the greatest celebrities in the world, Twain and his family reached New York on 15 October 1900, when they were greeted with fanfare and falderal. Livy refused to return to Hartford. No longer could she live in the home where Susy had died. They stayed in Manhattan, renting a house at 14 West 10th Street.

Twain resumed his friendship with Rogers and often went sailing on his yacht. He also renewed his friendship with Howells, who had left Boston for New York. Twain enjoyed the social opportunities the city offered but had trouble concentrating on his work. *Following the Equator* turned out to be the last major book Twain would publish. It was also his last subscription book. Though the loss of subscription publishing deprived Twain of his major source of income, it did offer a potential advantage: creative freedom. No longer would Twain have to write five-hundred-page illustrated books suitable for families. He had difficulty accepting the loss of the lucrative subscription book market, however. Living in New York, he socialized with the city's upper crust, often dining out and ignoring his work. Howells lamented, 'I hate to have him eating so many dinners, and writing so few books.'[17]

Given his celebrity, the magazines provided a forum for whatever Twain wished to say, but the magazine work he published around the turn of the century is fairly minor. Some consider 'The Man that Corrupted Hadleyburg', a 17,000-word story in the December 1899 issue of *Harper's*, the last masterpiece Twain published.

'The Man that Corrupted Hadleyburg' tells the story of a man wronged by a town whose residents see themselves as fine upstanding citizens incapable of corruption. Despite its critical reputation, the story is not without flaws. It goes on too long, and its bleak, angry tone can be offputting. Furthermore, its characters lack the individuality of Twain's finest creations. Like so much of Twain's later work, the story's emphasis on the selfish hypocrisy of humankind gets mired in misanthropy.

There may be no better way to recognize the story's problems than to read 'The Man that Corrupted Hadleyburg' in contrast with the story directly before it in the same issue of *Harper's*: Stephen Crane's 'Making an Orator', a bittersweet schoolroom tale that captures the pain teachers inflict when they force students to recite literature from memory. Whereas Twain's story is heavy-handed, Crane's possesses a light touch akin to Twain's earlier work. Jimmie Trescott, the boy in 'Making an Orator', is about Tom Sawyer's age. Whereas Tom wants everyone's attention, Jimmie prefers to blend into the background. Together Tom Sawyer and Jimmie Prescott provide two contrasting, yet equally valid versions of boyhood, both of which capture the joys and torments of growing up. 'The Man that Corrupted Hadleyburg', alternatively, depicts a bleak adult world devoid of either nostalgia for the past or promise for the future.

Henry Rogers's activities on his friend's behalf gave Twain more freedom to write. In 1903 Rogers negotiated a new agreement with Harper, making the firm Mark Twain's exclusive American publisher and severing his connection with American Publishing. The new agreement guaranteed Twain $25,000 annually, though his income generally exceeded that amount. It freed him from the pressure of writing piecemeal, but he did not use the opportunity to write slowly, patiently, meticulously, to craft a great new work of literature. Instead, he wrote short polemical pieces for the magazines that protested against Christian Science, imperialism, political corruption and vivisection.

Personal reasons partly explain Twain's inability to concentrate on his writing. Off and on throughout her life Livy had been sickly, but her health declined precipitously in late 1902. To improve her condition, Twain brought his wife and their two surviving daughters to Italy the following year. Isabel Lyon, whom Twain had hired as a personal secretary, soon joined them. They took a villa in Florence, where Livy endured until 5 June 1904, when her heart finally gave out. Twain and the girls returned home with the body, and Livy was buried in Elmira. Twain settled in Manhattan, renting a house at 21 Fifth Avenue. Suffering from nervous exhaustion brought about by her mother's death, Clara sought a rest cure. Jean stayed with their father for the time being, but her increasingly frequent seizures would put her into a sanatorium for a long stretch.

Isabel Lyon took on a much greater role in the household, serving as Twain's Girl Friday, managing the home and overseeing Jean's care. With Lyon's help, Twain resumed a major work he had started decades earlier. Intermittently since 1870 Twain had been attempting to write his autobiography. Having recommended to

Ned Wakeman that he dictate his personal story to a stenographer, Twain, with uneven results, had tried dictating as a method of composition himself. In Florence he returned to it. The new attempt was not ideal, since Lyon could not take shorthand, but Twain was convinced that spoken narrative was 'the right way to do an Autobiography'.[18]

The autobiography manifests Twain's obsession with how posterity would remember him. Writing it was one way for him

Mark Twain on the porch at Quarry Farm, photographic print, 1903.

Clara Clemens, undated, photographic print.

to shape the story of his life. Hiring an official biographer was another. In January 1906 Albert Bigelow Paine sought Twain's permission to write his biography. Twain was familiar with Paine's work. The two had corresponded when Paine was researching his biography of political cartoonist Thomas Nast, a copy of which he presented to Twain.[19] The book convinced him that its author had the right stuff to tackle his biography. Twain accepted the offer, gave Paine a room in his home, let him go through his manuscripts and permitted lengthy interviews.

When Paine arrived on 9 January 1906 to begin work, Josephine S. Hobby, an experienced stenographer, accompanied him. Hobby's presence convinced Twain to resume the autobiographical dictations he had begun in Florence. Most of that year Twain devoted to the autobiography. Typically, he would stay in bed, and Paine, Lyon and Hobby would enter his bedroom and listen to his horizontal dictations for a couple of hours every morning.

Instead of producing a chronological narrative, that is, an autobiography that starts with his birth and brings the story to the present, Twain used an innovative strategy of free association not dissimilar to the psychoanalytic method Sigmund Freud was developing simultaneously. A current event would trigger a memory of a time, place or person, whereupon Twain would develop that memory as fully as possible in his dictations. One memory often opened the door to many others.

News of the San Francisco earthquake, which took place on 18 April 1906, called to mind Twain's fond memories of the city. He remembered living with the Gillis family and frequenting the beer joints along Montgomery Street with Steve Gillis. These distant memories prompted him to relate his recent encounter with Richard Williams, Steve Gillis's nephew. Williams, then 37 years old, introduced himself as the eldest son of the eldest Gillis sister. 'Oh impossible,' Twain said, 'why they were nothing but young girls.' They grew up, Williams said, explaining the obvious. 'I see how it is,' Twain replied. 'Those young girls have remained young girls in my memory all this time.'[20] Twain exaggerated their youth to suit his autobiography, which frequently idealizes lost youth.

Though 1906 would be the most productive year for his autobiography, Twain would dictate additional chapters over the next three years. After selections from the work-in-progress began appearing in the *North American Review* in September 1906, Twain kept dictating. After he returned from a visit to England in 1907, where he had gone to accept an honorary degree from Oxford University, he resumed the dictations. And after he moved into 'Stormfield', the new mansion he built in Redding, Connecticut, he dictated further chapters.

Twain was unsure how to end the autobiography until his daughter Jean, at 29, died at Stormfield on 24 December 1909, a victim of Sudden Unexpected Death in Epilepsy (SUDEP). Her death prompted him to write a conclusion to the autobiography. Twain did not dictate 'The Death of Jean', as this section is also known, but wrote it out longhand, a therapeutic form of composition that helped him cope with the devastating loss. Jean's body was transported to Elmira to be buried with her mother and sister. Twain could not bring himself to make the trip. Instead he stayed home and kept writing 'The Death of Jean'. It was snowing on Christmas night when the hearse arrived at Stormfield. As it pulled away with its sad burden, Paine played a Schubert 'Impromptu' on the orchestrelle. The snow continued to fall.

Like the Gillis sisters, Twain's daughters typically appear in the autobiography as young girls. In one poignant section Twain recalls how he and Livy would reminisce about when their daughters were younger:

> We were always having vague dream-glimpses of them as they had used to be in the long-vanished years – glimpses of them playing and romping, with short frocks on, and spindle legs, and hair-tails down their backs – and always they were far and dim, and we could not hear their shouts and their laughter. How we longed to gather them to our arms! but they were only dainty and darling spectres, and they faded away and vanished, and left us desolate.[21]

Nearly all parents wax nostalgic for the time when their children were young, but Twain's nostalgia seems especially intense. The childhood of his daughters coincided with the richest and most productive period of his literary career. The period between the year Susy was born and the year Jean turned ten was also the period from 'Old Times on the Mississippi' to *Connecticut Yankee.* With Livy and the girls, Twain had a built-in audience for his work. Though he would remain in his study and write all day during their summers at Quarry Farm, in the evenings he would read what he had written to his wife and daughters, gauge their reaction and revise accordingly.[22]

With Isabel Lyon, Albert Bigelow Paine and Josephine Hobby, Twain had a new and different audience, but one suitable for the major work of his final years, the autobiography. Their presence helps explain some of its faults and imperfections. The autobiography is much too long. The modern edition fills three fat, closely printed volumes, topping out at over half a million words. It is also too self-indulgent. Though Lyon has been called Twain's 'other woman', she wasn't nearly as good an audience as Livy had been. Livy was unafraid to criticize her husband's writings. Lyon lacked her boldness, strength of character and critical acumen. She adored her employer – 'the King', she called him – and found it impossible to criticize anything he wrote.[23]

Paine, too, had trouble criticizing Twain's autobiographical excesses. In his role as official biographer – hagiographer, one might say – Paine knew that the longer the autobiography was, the more material he would have for his biography. Like Lyon, Paine took the autobiography as it came from Twain's mouth. Recognizing Lyon, Paine and Hobby as the overindulgent audience for his dictations is essential for understanding Twain's fascinating but all-too-often flawed autobiography.

The idea of audience provides the key to appreciating Twain's earlier literary career, as well. When he wrote 'The Dandy and the Squatter' at sixteen, he had a good understanding of his audience, which consisted of people who read humorous newspaper sketches, the same people who were reading the work of other contemporary humorists. In Nevada and California he belonged to a community of male journalists who enjoyed the rollicking humour that characterizes Twain's Western tales and sketches.

Twain's finest novels – *Tom Sawyer*, *Huckleberry Finn* and *Connecticut Yankee* – achieve a rare synthesis: they straddle a dual audience, lovers of Old Southwest humour and genteel, mainstream readers. As an author, Twain was at his best when he combined different genres of literature – sentimental fiction, science fiction, the utopian novel, travel writing, autobiography – with the themes, motifs, techniques and humour of the Old Southwest.

Having entered the world with Halley's Comet, Twain predicted he would leave the same way. The coincidence, he thought, would make a kind of weird symmetry. In addition, the appearance of Halley's Comet at his death would provide cosmic affirmation of his literary greatness. As Calpurnia says in *Julius Caesar*: 'When beggars die there are no comets seen; / The heavens themselves blaze forth the death of princes.' Halley's Comet returned in 1910, reaching its perihelion on 20 April 1910. Beset by severe chest pains, largely due to a lifetime of cigar smoking, Mark Twain died the following day. Astride the comet he escaped the darkness.

References

Introduction

1 Henry Miller, *The Books in My Life* (New York, 1969), pp. 41, 318; Henry Miller, *The Colossus of Maroussi* [1941] (New York, 2010), pp. 115–16.

2 Henry Miller, *The Time of the Assassins: A Study of Rimbaud* (New York, 1962), p. 162; Miller, *Books in My Life*, p. 255.

3 H. L. Mencken, 'From the Diary of a Reviewer', *Smart Set*, LXVI (1921), p. 142; Ernest Hemingway, *Green Hills of Africa* (New York, 1935), p. 22; SLC to Henry Huttleston Rogers, 26–8 April 1897, in *Correspondence with Henry Huttleston Rogers, 1893–1909*, ed. Lewis Leary (Berkeley, CA, 1969), p. 274.

4 Kevin J. Hayes, *A Journey through American Literature* (Oxford, 2012), p. 155.

5 Hemingway, *Green Hills*, p. 22; Leonard Woolf, 'Mark Twain', *Nation and the Athenaeum*, 26 September 1925, p. 765; *The Paris Review Interviews* (New York, 2006), vol. I, p. 127.

6 Waldo Frank, *Our America* (New York, 1919), p. 38; Ray Froman, 'Charlie Chaplin', in *Charlie Chaplin: Interviews*, ed. Kevin J. Hayes (Jackson, MS, 2005), p. 44; Charles Chaplin, *My Autobiography* (Harmondsworth, 1966), p. 245.

7 T. S. Eliot, 'Introduction to the *Adventures of Huckleberry Finn*', in *Huckleberry Finn: Text, Sources, Criticism*, ed. Kenneth S. Lynn (New York, 1961), p. 199.

8 Kenneth Rexroth, 'Huckleberry Finn', *Saturday Review*, 13 May 1967, p. 14.

9 Ibid., p. 15.

10 Norman Mailer, 'Huckleberry Finn, Alive at 100', *New York Times*, 9 December 1984, p. A1+; Waldo Frank, 'Emerging Greatness', *Seven Arts*, November 1916, p. 78.

11 George Orwell, *Complete Works* (London, 1986), vol. XVI, p. 5.

12 Harriet Monroe, 'A Nation-wide Art', *Poetry*, VII (1915), 84; Simone de Beauvoir, *America Day by Day*, trans. Carol Cosman (Berkeley, CA, 1999), p. 216.

13 Cyril Clemens, *An Evening with A. E. Housman* (Webster Groves, MO, 1937), pp. 9, 15; Robin Skynner and John Cleese, *Life and How to Survive It: An Entertaining and Mind-stretching Search for What Really Matters in Life* (New York, 1996), p. 214.

14 Robert C. Benchley, *Love Conquers All* (New York, 1922), p. 303; Leonard Woolf, 'Mark Twain', *Nation and the Athenaeum*, 8 November 1924, p. 217; Robert Benchley, 'For Release Monday: Autobiographical Disclosures in the Informal Manner', *Bookman* (March 1925), pp. 43–6.

15 Richard Aldington, 'Mark Twain', *Spectator*, 29 November 1924, p. 830.

16 Mark Twain, *Mark Twain in Eruption: Hitherto Unpublished Pages about Men and Events*, ed. Bernard De Voto (New York, 1940); Mark Twain, *The Autobiography of Mark Twain*, ed. Charles Neider (New York, 1959); James D. Brasch and Joseph Sigman, *Hemingway's Library: A Composite Record* (New York, 1981), nos 1343, 1345.

17 Tim Adams, 'Twain's World: Still Fresh, 100 Years On', *Observer*, 21 November 2010, p. 35; Garrison Keillor, 'Riverboat Rambler', *New York Times*, 19 December 2010, p. 7.

18 Mark Twain, *The Tragedy of Pudd'nhead Wilson and the Comedy Those Extraordinary Twins* (Hartford, CT, 1894), p. 179.

19 Mark Twain, *Autobiography of Mark Twain*, ed. Harriet Elinor Smith (Berkeley, 2010–15) (hereafter, *Autobiography*), vol. I, p. 459.

20 *Mark Twain's Notebook*, ed. Albert Bigelow Paine (New York, 1935), p. 345.

21 Mark Twain, *Roughing It*, ed. Harriet Elinor Smith and Edgar Marquess Branch (Berkeley, CA, 1993) (hereafter, *Roughing It*), p. 276.

22 *Autobiography*, vol. I, p. 22.

1 The Old Southwest

1 *Autobiography*, vol. i, p. 64; Thomas V. Bodine, 'Monroe County', in *A History of Northeast Missouri*, ed. Walter Williams (Chicago, il, 1913), vol. i, p. 465.

2 James H. Justus, *Fetching the Old Southwest: Humorous Writing from Longstreet to Twain* (Columbia, mo, 2004), pp. 77–114.

3 *Roughing It*, p. 271; Mark Twain, *The Tragedy of Pudd'nhead Wilson and the Comedy Those Extraordinary Twins* (Hartford, ct, 1894), p. 156.

4 Dixon Wecter, *Sam Clemens of Hannibal* (Boston, ma, 1952), p. 9.

5 *Autobiography*, vol. i, p. 452.

6 Wecter, *Sam Clemens*, pp. 33–4.

7 *Autobiography*, vol. i, p. 64.

8 Wecter, *Sam Clemens*, p. 40; *Autobiography*, vol. i, p. 215; 'Spanked Twain', *Burlington [ia] Gazette*, 2 December 1895; Mark Twain, *Hannibal, Huck and Tom*, ed. Walter Blair (Berkeley, ca, 1969), p. 52.

9 Ibid.

10 Mark Twain, *How to Tell a Story and Other Essays* (Hartford, ct, 1901), p. 8.

11 *Autobiography*, vol. i, pp. 210, 216.

12 'Mark Twain's Chum', *New York Press*, 28 January 1900, p. 27; *Autobiography*, vol. i, p. 211.

13 *Autobiography*, vol. i, p. 217.

14 Edgar Allan Poe, *The Annotated Poe*, ed. Kevin J. Hayes (Cambridge, ma, 2015), p. 58.

15 Twain, *How to Tell a Story*, p. 12.

16 *Autobiography*, vol. i, p. 217.

17 Mark Twain, *Early Tales and Sketches*, ed. Edgar Marquess Branch and Robert H. Hirst (Berkeley, ca, 1979), vol. i, p. 64.

18 Mark Twain, *The Adventures of Tom Sawyer*, ed. John C. Gerber and Paul Baender (Berkeley, ca, 1982), p. 10; *Adventures of Huckleberry Finn*, ed. Victor Fischer and Lin Salamo (Berkeley, ca, 2003), p. 137.

19 Mark Twain, *The Innocents Abroad; or, The New Pilgrims' Progress* (Hartford, ct, 1869), p. 169.

20 Ibid., p. 177.

21 Twain, *Hannibal, Huck and Tom*, p. 29; *Autobiography*, vol. i, p. 418.

22 *Autobiography*, vol. i, p. 418.

23 Twain, *Innocents Abroad*, p. 492.

24 Mark Twain, *Notebooks and Journals*, ed. Frederick Anderson et al. (Berkeley, CA, 1975–9) (hereafter, *Notebooks*), vol. I, p. 37; Samuel Langhorne Clemens (hereafter, SLC) to Jane Lampton Clemens, 20 March 1862, in *Letters*, ed. Edgar Marquess Branch et al. (Berkeley, CA, 1988–) (hereafter, *Letters*), vol. I, p. 175.

25 Twain, *Hannibal, Huck and Tom*, p. 34; SLC to Olivia L. Langdon, 2 March 1869, in *Letters*, vol. III, p. 132; Alan Gribben, *Mark Twain's Library: A Reconstruction* (Boston, MA, 1980) (hereafter, Gribben), vol. II, p. 679.

26 Twain, *Innocents Abroad*, p. 411.

27 'Schoolmate of Mark Twain', *Worth County Index* [Northwood, IA], 18 February 1909, p. 2.

28 Wecter, *Sam Clemens*, p. 140.

29 *Autobiography*, vol. I, pp. 351, 397.

30 Henrietta Cosgrove, 'Mark Twain's Boyhood', *Fort Wayne Daily Gazette*, 8 April 1885, p. 7. This interview first appeared anonymously in the *Chicago Inter-Ocean*, 5 April 1885; the *Gazette* editor identified Cosgrove, a personal friend, as the interviewer.

31 Ibid.

32 Wecter, *Sam Clemens*, pp. 201–2.

33 *Autobiography*, vol. I, p. 355.

34 Menahem Blondheim, *News Over the Wires: The Telegraph and the Flow of Public Information in America, 1844–1897* (Cambridge, MA, 1994), p. 56; Richard B. Kielbowicz, *News in the Mail: The Press, Post Office, and Public Information, 1700–1860s* (New York, 1989), p. 149.

35 J. A. Leo Lemay, 'The Origins of the Humor of the Old South', in *The Humor of the Old South*, ed. M. Thomas Inge and Edward J. Piacentino (Lexington, KY, 2001), p. 13.

36 Wecter, *Sam Clemens*, p. 246; Frank Luther Mott, *A History of American Magazines, 1850–1865* (Cambridge, MA, 1938), p. 181.

37 'The Dandy Frightening the Squatter', *Rockland County* [NY] *Journal*, 17 July 1852; 'Drilling Key Holes', *Onondaga* [NY] *Gazette*, 26 August 1852.

38 'Didn't Scare Him Bad', *Kentucky Tribune*, 9 September 1853. Under the title 'Fighting a Squatter', the story appeared in *Cooper's Clarksburg* [VA, later WV] *Register*, 27 December 1854; *Nashville* [TN] *Parlor Visitor*, July 1854 (cited in the following item); Greenville, SC, *Southern Enterprise*,

25 March 1858; Charlotte, NC, *Western Democrat*, 13 April 1858; *Geneva* [NY] *Gazette*, 15 October 1858; and *Bedford* [PA] *Gazette*, 31 December 1858. Under the title 'Frightening a Squatter', it appeared in Washington, DC, *Daily American Organ*, 25 March 1856; Raleigh, NC, *Spirit of the Age*, 26 March 1856; *Port Tobacco Times and Charles County* [MD] *Advertiser*, 3 April 1856 and 18 December 1856; Elkton, MD, *Cecil Whig*, 12 April 1856; *Rockland County* [NY] *Journal*, 3 May 1856; *Fayetteville* [TN] *Observer*, 2 October 1856; Ellicotsville, NY, *American Union*, 8 October 1858; and Atchison, KS, *Freedom's Champion*, 7 September 1861. 'Didn't Scare Him Bad', *Gallipolis* [OH] *Journal*, 16 April 1863.

39 Twain, *Early Tales*, vol. I, pp. 64–5.

40 Timothy C. Frazer, 'A Note on Mark Twain's Use of Dialect in Earlier Writings', *Mark Twain Journal*, XX (1980), p. 8.

41 Mark Twain, 'Old Times on the Mississippi', *Atlantic* (January 1875), p. 70.

42 *Autobiography*, vol. I, p. 460.

43 SLC to Jane Lampton Clemens, 24 August 1853, and SLC to Jane Lampton Clemens and Pamela A. Moffett, 1 June 1863, in *Letters*, vol. I, pp. 3, 5, 256.

44 SLC to Jane Lampton Clemens, 31 August 1853, in *Letters*, vol. I, p. 10.

45 SLC to Orion Clemens, 28 November 1853, in *Letters*, vol. I, p. 29.

46 SLC to the Muscatine *Journal*, 17–18 February 1854, in *Letters*, vol. I, p. 40.

47 Gribben, vol. I, p. 44.

48 Twain, *Early Tales*, vol. I, pp. 111–17.

49 William E. Curtis, 'Mark Twain Out West', *Ironwood* [MI] *Times*, 16 August 1888, p. 3.

50 Gribben, vol. I, p. 310; Mark Twain, *What is Man? and Other Philosophical Writings*, ed. Paul Baender (Berkeley, CA, 1973), p. 459.

51 Cosgrove, 'Mark Twain's Boyhood', p. 7.

52 Thomas Bangs Thorpe, 'The Big Bear of Arkansas', *Spirit of the Times*, 27 March 1841, p. 43; Mark Twain, *Mississippi Writings*, ed. Guy Cardwell (New York, 1982), p. 344.

53 Ibid., p. 275.

54 Ibid., pp. 283–4.

55 Edgar Marquess Branch, *Men Call Me Lucky: Mark Twain and the Pennsylvania* (Oxford, OH, 1985), pp. 31–9.

56 'A Story of Mark Twain', *Gloversville* [NY] *Daily Leader,* 30 August 1902, p. 2.

57 Twain, *Mississippi Writings*, p. 284.

58 Twain, *Early Tales*, vol. I, p. 149.

59 Twain, *Mississippi Writings*, p. 313.

60 'M'me Caprell', *New Orleans Daily Crescent*, 10 December 1860; SLC to Orion and Mary E. Clemens, 6 February 1861, in *Letters*, vol. I, p. 108.

2 Doings in Nevada

1 Mark Twain, 'The Private History of a Campaign that Failed', *Century*, XXXI (1885), pp. 193–204.

2 *Roughing It*, p. 30.

3 Ibid., pp. 120–21.

4 Ibid., pp. 154–6.

5 Mark Twain, *The Innocents Abroad; or, The New Pilgrims' Progress* (Hartford, CT, 1869), p. 284; SLC to Jane Lampton Clemens, 30 January 1862, in *Letters*, vol. I, p. 147.

6 George Ade, 'Mark Twain as Our Emissary', *Century*, LXXXI (1910), p. 205; SLC to Orion Clemens, 17–19 April 1862, in *Letters*, vol. I, p. 190; Gribben, vol. I, p. 189.

7 Mark Twain, *Hannibal, Huck and Tom*, ed. Walter Blair (Berkeley, CA, 1969), p. 35.

8 Lawrence I. Berkove, 'Goodman, Joseph Thompson', in *American National Biography*, ed. John Arthur Garraty and Mark Christopher Carnes (Oxford, 1999), vol. IX, p. 244; 'People and Politics', *San Bernardino Daily Sun*, 23 April 1907, p. 10.

9 'The Insider', *San Francisco Call*, 7 December 1908, p. 6.

10 Lawrence I. Berkove, 'De Quille, Dan', *American National Biography*, vol. VI, p. 463.

11 SLC to Orion Clemens, 22 June 1862, in *Letters*, vol. I, p. 221.

12 Mark Twain, *Early Tales and Sketches*, ed. Edgar Marquess Branch and Robert H. Hirst (Berkeley, CA, 1979), vol. I, p. 16.

13 Lawrence I. Berkove, 'Daggett, Rollin Mallory', in *American National Biography*, vol. VI, p. 3.

14 Ron Hohenhaus, 'The "Petrified Man" Returns: An Early Mark Twain Hoax Makes an Unexpected Appearance in Australasia', *Australasian Journal of American Studies*, XXVII (2008), pp. 83–103; 'Petrified Man', *Fremont Journal*, 21 November 1862.

15 Twain, *Early Tales*, vol. I, p. 159.

16 Ibid., p. 170; Joseph L. Coulombe, *Mark Twain and the American West* (Columbia, MO, 2003), p. 101.

17 Twain, *Early Tales*, vol. I, p. 173.

18 Ibid., p. 174.

19 J. T. Goodman to Albert Bigelow Paine, 11 June 1907, in 'Goodman's Assistance on the Biography', *Twainian*, XV (1956), p. 2; Alan Lessoff, 'Stewart, William Morris', in *American National Biography*, vol. XX, p. 756; William M. Stewart, *Reminiscences of Senator William M. Stewart of Nevada*, ed. George Rothwell Brown (Washington, DC, 1908), p. 220.

20 Stewart, *Reminiscences*, p. 221.

21 SLC to Jane Lampton Clemens and Pamela A. Moffett, 11–12 April and 18 July 1863, in *Letters*, vol. I, pp. 248, 261.

22 Twain, *Early Tales*, vol. I, p. 228.

23 'Reportorial', Marysville *Daily Appeal*, 28 February 1863; 'Reportorial', Portland *Morning Oregonian*, 14 March 1863.

24 Twain, *Early Tales*, vol. I, p. 253.

25 'Unfortunate Blunder', *Sonoma County Democrat*, 12 September 1863.

26 Twain, *Early Tales*, vol. I, p. 298.

27 'Curing a Cold', *Oxford Benton Tribune*, 30 May 1867.

28 Dan De Quille, 'Salad Days of Mark Twain', in *The Life and Times of the Virginia City Territorial Enterprise: Being Reminiscences of Five Distinguished Comstock Journalists*, ed. Oscar Lewis (Ashland, OR, 1971), p. 38.

29 *Notebooks*, vol. II, p. 510; Alfred H. Marks, 'Browne, Charles Farrar', in *American National Biography*, vol. III, p. 755.

30 SLC to Jane Lampton Clemens, 2? January 1864, in *Letters*, vol. I, p. 268.

31 Mark Twain, *Mark Twain of the Enterprise: Newspaper Articles and Other Documents, 1862–1864*, ed. Henry Nash Smith and Frederick Anderson (Berkeley, CA, 1957), p. 123.

32 J. T. Goodman to Albert Bigelow Paine, 7 April 1911 and 18 February 1907, in 'Goodman's Assistance', pp. 4, 2; Twain, *Early Tales*, vol. II, p. 10.

33 SLC to Orion and Mary E. Clemens, 28 September 1864, in *Letters*, vol. I, p. 315.

34 Twain, *Early Tales*, vol. II, p. 110.

35 Ibid., p. 128.

36 Ibid., pp. 132–3.

37 *Autobiography*, vol. II, p. 113; 'The Insider', *San Francisco Call*, 7 December 1908, p. 6.

38 William R. Gillis, *Memories of Mark Twain and Steve Gillis* (Sonora, CA, 1924), pp. 29–30.

3 The View from Jackass Hill

1 *Autobiography*, vol. III, p. 58; *Notebooks*, vol. I, p. 69.

2 *Autobiography*, vol. II, p. 422 and vol. III, pp. 58–60; *Roughing It*, p. 416.

3 *Notebooks*, vol. I, p. 70; Dan De Quille, 'Old-time Gold Delvers', *Daily Alta California*, 22 March 1885, p. 1; Lawrence I. Berkove, 'Jim Gillis: "The Thoreau of the Sierras"', *Mark Twain Circular*, II/3–4 (1988), p. 2.

4 *Autobiography*, vol. III, p. 57.

5 *Roughing It*, p. 419.

6 *Autobiography*, vol. III, p. 58.

7 John Seelye, *The True Adventures of Huckleberry Finn* (New York, 1971), p. 238.

8 SLC to James N. Gillis, 26 January 1870, in *Letters*, vol. IV, p. 36; *Notebooks*, vol. I, pp. 70, 80.

9 Henry J. W. Dam, 'A Morning with Bret Harte', in *Twain in His Own Time*, ed. Gary Scharnhorst (Iowa City, IA, 2010), p. 52.

10 Mark Twain, *Early Tales and Sketches*, ed. Edgar Marquess Branch and Robert H. Hirst (Berkeley, CA, 1979), vol. II, p. 283.

11 'Podgers' Letter from New York', *Daily Alta California*, 10 January 1866, p. 1.

12 'Jim Smiley', Cleveland *Daily Leader*, 7 January 1866.

13 Twain, *Early Tales*, vol. II, p. 362.

14 Ibid., p. 364.

15 Tony Tanner, *The Reign of Wonder: Naivety and Reality in American Literature* (Cambridge, 1965), p. 130.

16 Mark Twain, *Letters from Hawaii*, ed. A. Grove Day (New York, 1966), pp. 3–4.

17 Ibid., p. 168.

18 *Autobiography*, vol. I, p. 227.

19 SLC to Elisha Bliss, Jr, 7 September 1869, and to Olivia L. Langdon, 18 December 1869, in *Letters*, vol. III, pp. 340, 431; Goodman, quoted in David H. Fears, *Mark Twain Day by Day: An Annotated Chronology of the Life of Samuel L. Clemens* (Banks, OR, 2008–13), vol. I, p. 926.

20 *Roughing It*, p. 542.

21 Mark Twain, 'Letter from "Mark Twain"', *Daily Alta California*, 18 January 1867.

22 *Autobiography*, vol. II, p. 192.

23 Ibid., vol. III, p. 114.

24 Ibid., vol. II, p. 47.

25 William Webster Ellsworth, *A Golden Age of Authors: A Publisher's Recollection* (Boston, MA, 1919), p. 222; Eleanor Melville Metcalf, *Herman Melville: Cycle and Epicycle* (Cambridge, MA, 1953), p. 185.

26 L. Anne Clark Doherty, 'Webb, Charles Henry', in *American National Biography*, ed. John Arthur Garraty and Mark Christopher Carnes (Oxford, 1999), vol. XXII, p. 841; John Paul, *pseud.* [Charles Webb], 'Advertisement', *The Celebrated Jumping Frog of Calaveras County, and Other Sketches* (London, 1867), p. v.

27 Jacob Blanck, *Bibliography of American Literature* (New Haven, CT, 1955–91), no. 7095; Gribben, vol. I, p. 295; 'Letter from "Mark Twain"', *Daily Alta California*, 14 July 1867, p. 1.

28 'The Citizen's Book Table', *New York Citizen*, 4 May 1867, reprinted in Louis J. Budd, ed., *Mark Twain: The Contemporary Reviews* (New York, 1999) (hereafter, Budd), p. 26.

29 'New Books', *Philadelphia Inquirer*, 6 May 1867, p. 2; 'Literature', Philadelphia *Daily Evening Telegraph*, 18 May 1867, p. 7 (neither in Budd).

30 'Mark Twain's Lecture', *Anglo-American Times*, 1 June 1867, p. 11 (not in Budd).

31 'Californian Humour', *London Review*, 21 September 1867, 330 (cited, but not reprinted, in Budd, p. 31).

32 James N. Cox, *Mark Twain: The Fate of Humor* (Princeton, NJ, 1966), pp. 13, 19.

33 [Thomas Hood,] 'Our Library Table', *Fun*, 19 October 1867, p. 65 (reprinted, without attribution, in Budd, pp. 30–31).

34 [Thomas Hood,] 'Here, There, and Everywhere', *Fun*, 13 November 1869, p. 95 (not in Budd).

35 Jonathan Rose, *The Intellectual Life of the British Working Classes* (New Haven, CT, 2001), p. 84.

36 'Kibworth', *Leicester Chronicle*, 26 October 1867, p. 6.

37 'Myrniong', *Bacchus Marsh Express*, 26 December 1868, p. 3.

38 'Lyttelton Winter Readings', Christchurch *Star*, 8 October 1870; 'Local and General', *Dunstan Times*, 8 July 1870.

39 'Kaiapoi Winter Entertainment', Christchurch *Star*, 29 July 1869; 'The Penny Readings', *Cheltenham Chronicle*, 10 December 1867, p. 5; 'The Popular Readings', *Melvor Times and Rodney Advertiser*, 9 October 1868, p. 2.

4 *The Innocents Abroad*

1 SLC to Jane Lampton Clemens, 15 April 1867, in *Letters*, vol. II, pp. 23–4.

2 SLC to Jane Lampton Clemens, 1 June 1867, in *Letters*, vol. II, p. 50.

3 *Notebooks*, vol. I, p. 330.

4 Mark Twain, *The Innocents Abroad: or, The New Pilgrims' Progress* (Hartford, CT, 1869), p. 29.

5 Dewey Ganzel, *Mark Twain Abroad: The Cruise of the Quaker City* (Chicago, IL, 1968), pp. 27–8.

6 Bloodgood H. Cutter, *The Long Island Farmer's Poems: Lines Written on the Quaker City Excursion to Palestine, and Other Poems* (New York, 1886), p. 7.

7 *Roughing It*, p. 154.

8 Gribben, vol. I, p. 168.

9 Twain, *Innocents Abroad*, p. 50.

10 SLC to Jane Lampton Clemens, 2 July 1867, in *Letters*, vol. II, p. 68.

11 Cutter, *Long Island Farmer's Poems*, p. 27.

12 Twain, *Innocents Abroad*, p. 126.

13 Ibid., p. 190.

14 Ibid., p. 215.

15 Ibid., p. 290.

16 Ibid., p. 221.

17 Richard Garvey to SLC, 7 July 1884, in *Dear Mark Twain: Letters from His Readers*, ed. R. Kent Rasmussen (Berkeley, CA, 2013), p. 105.

18 Cutter, *Long Island Farmer's Poems*, p. 48.

19 Mark Twain, *Mark Twain Speaking*, ed. Paul Fatout (Iowa City, IA, 1976), p. 33.

20 Twain, *Innocents Abroad*, pp. 375–6.

21 Ibid., pp. 451–2.

22 *Notebooks*, vol. I, p. 472.

23 Twain, *Innocents Abroad*, p. 567.

24 'Twainiana', New York *World*, 10 December 1899, p. 3.

25 *Complete Interviews*, pp. 15–16.

26 SLC to John Russell Young, 22 November 1867, in *Letters*, vol. II, pp. 108–9.

27 SLC to Elisha Bliss, Jr., 2 December 1867, and to Frank Fuller, 5 December 1867, in *Letters*, vol. II, pp. 119, 128.

28 Mark Twain, 'The Holy Land Excursion', *Daily Alta California*, 29 October 1867; Mark Twain, 'Turkish Lunch', Rock Island *Daily Argus*, 15 June 1868; '"Mark Twain" on a Turkish Lunch', *Flake's Semi-weekly Galveston Bulletin*, 25 December 1867, p. 7; 'Mark Twain's Turkish Lunch', *Bangor Daily Whig and Courier*, 23 January 1868.

29 SLC to Elisha Bliss, Jr, 2 December 1867, in *Letters*, vol. II, p. 119; Keith Arbour, 'Book Canvassers, Mark Twain and Hamlet's Ghost', *PBSA*, XCIII (1999), p. 8.

30 Annie Nelles, *Annie Nelles; or, The Life of a Book Agent: An Autobiography* (Cincinnati, OH, 1868), p. 254.

31 Mark Twain, *Satires and Burlesques*, ed. Franklin R. Rogers (Berkeley, CA, 1967), p. 56.

32 Ibid.

33 Arbour, 'Book Canvassers', p. 17; Nelles, *Annie Nelles*, p. 258; Twain, *Satires and Burlesques*, p. 56.

34 [Harriet Wasson], *Facts by a Woman* (Oakland, CA, 1881), p. 35.

35 William M. Stewart, *Reminiscences of Senator William M. Stewart of Nevada*, ed. George Rothwell Brown (Washington, DC, 1908), pp. 219–20.

36 *Notebooks*, vol. I, p. 488. Twain's abbreviated note has been expanded for clarity.

37 SLC to Jane Lampton Clemens, 8 January 1868, in *Letters*, vol. II, p. 144.

38 *Autobiography*, vol. i, p. 320; vol. iii, p. 165.

39 'Contract for *The Innocents Abroad*', in *Letters*, vol. ii, p. 421.

40 SLC to Emeline B. Beach, 10 February 1868, in *Letters*, vol. ii, p. 183.

41 Mark Twain, *'Coming Out': A Letter to a Rosebud of Two Generations Ago Now Inscribed to a Bud of Today from the Same Shoot* (New York, 1921), p. 10.

42 H.J.R., 'Where, How and Why "Mark Twain" Wrote His *Innocents Abroad* in Washington', New York *Daily Graphic*, 25 January 1883.

43 SLC to Mary Mason Fairbanks, 5 May 1868, in *Letters*, vol. ii, p. 212.

44 SLC to Charles Henry Webb, 26 November 1870, in *Letters*, vol. iv, p. 248.

45 SLC to Elisha Bliss, Jr, 28 May 1868, in *Letters*, vol. ii, p. 218; 'Review', *North-China Herald*, 29 June 1872, p. 518 (not in Budd).

46 SLC to Olivia L. Langdon, 20 January 1869, in *Letters*, vol. iii, pp. 51–2.

47 'Mark Twain's Lecture', Toledo *Blade*, 21 January 1869, reprinted in *Letters*, vol. iii, p. 457.

48 *Autobiography*, vol. i, p. 147; SLC to Olivia L. Langdon, 10 March 1869, in *Letters*, vol. iii, p. 158.

49 'Book Agents Wanted', *Defiance Democrat*, 25 September 1869.

50 SLC to Olivia L. Langdon, 7 September 1869, in *Letters*, vol. iii, p. 345.

51 'Literary Matters', Toledo *Commercial*, 3 September 1869 (reprinted in Budd, p. 55).

52 SLC to Elisha Bliss, 28 January 1870, in *Letters*, vol. iv, p. 40.

53 W. D. Howells, *Literary Friends and Acquaintance: A Personal Retrospect of American Authorship*, ed. David F. Hiatt and Edwin H. Cady (Bloomington, IN, 1968), p. 257.

54 [Thomas Hood,] 'Turning over New Leaves', *Fun*, 10 September 1870, p. 104; 'The New Pilgrim's Progress', *Examiner and London Review*, 26 November 1870, p. 758; 'A Humorist's Travels in the East', *Field*, 24 December 1870, p. 556 (none in Budd).

55 'Conrad Pays Tribute to Mark Twain', *Mentor*, May 1924, p. 45.

56 Mark Twain, 'The Late Benjamin Franklin', in *Benjamin Franklin*, ed. Kevin J. Hayes (New York, 2008), p. 55.

57 SLC to James N. Gillis, 26 January 1870, in *Letters*, vol. iv, p. 35.

58 SLC to Joseph H. and Harmony C. Twichell, 12 November 1870, in *Letters*, vol. iv, p. 237.

5 The River

1 SLC to Jane Lampton Clemens and Pamela A. Moffett, 6 February 1868, in *Letters*, vol. II, p. 179.

2 'Mark Twain on His Travels', *Daily Alta California*, 3 March 1868.

3 See, for example, Jerome Loving, *Mark Twain: The Adventures of Samuel L. Clemens* (Berkeley, CA, 2010), p. 185.

4 SLC to Olivia L. Clemens, 27 November 1871, in *Letters*, vol. IV, p. 499.

5 *The Ohio Guide* (New York, 1940), p. 319; SLC to Olivia L. Clemens, 19 January 1872, *Letters*, vol. V, p. 15.

6 *Roughing It*, p. xxiv; Karl Kron, *Ten Thousand Miles on a Bicycle* (New York, 1887), p. iv; 'Current Literature', *Overland Monthly*, VIII (1872), p. 581 (Budd, p. 107); Henrietta Cosgrove, 'Mark Twain's Boyhood', Fort Wayne *Daily Gazette*, 8 April 1885, p. 7.

7 David H. Fears, *Mark Twain Day by Day* (Banks, OR, 2008–13), vol. I, p. 379.

8 SLC to Susy Clemens, 9 May 1872, in *Letters*, vol. V, p. 85.

9 Mark Twain, *The Adventures of Tom Sawyer: A Facsimile of the Author's Holograph Manuscript*, ed. Paul Baender (Washington, DC, 1982), vol. I, p. 23.

10 Mark Twain, 'A Family Sketch', *A Family Sketch and Other Private Writings*, ed. Benjamin Griffin (Berkeley, CA, 2014), pp. 42–3.

11 SLC to William Dean Howells, 2 September 1874, in *Letters*, vol. VI, p. 217; Molly Sinclair, 'Mother and Son's Amazing Reunion', *Washington Post*, 27 February 1986, p. Md.1.

12 Mark Twain, 'A True Story, Repeated Word for Word as I Heard It', *Atlantic* (November 1874), p. 592.

13 Lee Smith, 'Introduction', Mark Twain, *Sketches, New and Old* (Oxford, 1996), p. xl.

14 SLC to Joseph H. and Harmony C. Twichell, 11 June 1874, in *Letters*, vol. VI, p. 158.

15 SLC to Edgar Wakeman, 25 April 1874, in *Letters*, vol. VI, p. 119.

16 *Autobiography*, vol. II, p. 196.

17 SLC to Emma Parish, 20 September 1874, and to Olivia Lewis Langdon, 24 September 1874, in *Letters*, vol. VI, pp. 237, 245.

18 *Complete Interviews*, p. 2.

19 SLC to Olivia L. Clemens, 12 November 1874, in *Letters*, vol. VI, pp. 277–8.

20 W. D. Howells, *Literary Friends and Acquaintance: A Personal Retrospect of American Authorship*, ed. David F. Hiatt and Edwin H. Cady (Bloomington, IN, 1968), p. 284.

21 'The Mississippi Pilot', Launceston *Tasmanian*, 6 October 1877, p. 10 (not in Budd).

22 'Conrad Pays Tribute to Mark Twain', *Mentor*, May 1924, p. 45.

23 John C. Gerber et al., 'Introduction', *The Adventures of Tom Sawyer*, ed. John C. Gerber et al. (Berkeley, CA, 1980), p. 16.

24 Under the title 'How Tom Sawyer Got His Fence Whitewashed', the extract appeared in several Australian papers, including *Sydney Mail and New South Wales Advertiser*, 2 September 1876, p. 7; *Glen Innes Examiner and General Advertiser*, 13 September 1876, p. 3; *Goulburn Herald and Chronicle*, 28 October 1876, p. 2; *Alexandria Times*, 11 November 1876, p. 3; and Brisbane *Week*, 2 June 1877, p. 24. Under the same title, the extract appeared in the Nelson, New Zealand, *Colonist*, 28 September 1876.

25 'The Bohemian Book-worm', *Penny Illustrated Paper and Illustrated Times*, 24 June 1876, p. 414; 'Mark Twain's New Book', *Examiner*, 17 June 1876, pp. 684–5 (neither in Budd).

26 'Tom Sawyer', London *Morning Post*, 18 September 1876, p. 3 (not in Budd).

27 'Child's Popular Ballads', *Saturday Review*, 24 October 1885, p. 551; 'Members of the American Folklore Society', *Journal of American Folklore*, 1 (1888), p. 94.

28 Gordon Roper, 'Mark Twain and His Canadian Publishers', *American Book Collector*, X (1960), p. 19; [Harriet Wasson], *Facts by a Woman* (Oakland, CA, 1881), pp. 42, 45.

29 [Wasson], *Facts by a Woman*, pp. 53–5.

30 Gerber et al., 'Introduction', p. 29.

31 Hershel Parker, 'Historical Supplement', Herman Melville, *Clarel: A Poem and Pilgrimage in the Holy Land*, ed. Harrison Hayford et al. (Evanston, IL, 1991), p. 659.

32 *Mark Twain's Notebook*, ed. Albert Bigelow Paine (New York, 1935), p. 190.

33 Wallace Martin, *Recent Theories of Narrative* (Ithaca, NY, 1986), p. 69.

34 Kevin J. Hayes, *A Journey through American Literature* (Oxford, 2012), pp. 10–11.

35 Mark Twain, *Adventures of Huckleberry Finn*, ed. Victor Fischer et al. (Berkeley, CA, 2003), p. 109.

36 Ibid., pp. 119, 121.

37 Twain, 'Family Sketch', p. 43.

38 Twain, *Adventures of Huckleberry Finn*, p. 65.

39 'Received at Reading Rooms', *California Farmer*, 18 April 1878, p. 196; Jacob Blanck, *Bibliography of American Literature* (New Haven, CT, 1955–91), no. 3378; 'Mark Twain's Scrap Book', *Indiana* [PA] *Democrat*, 14 November 1878.

40 Kron, *Ten Thousand Miles*, pp. 356–7.

41 Ibid., p. 640.

42 *Notebooks*, vol. I, p. 346.

43 J. W. Sherman, 'Why Do Doctors Disagree in Diagnosis?', *Massachusetts Medical Journal*, VII (1887), p. 202.

44 *Mark Twain Speaking*, ed. Paul Fatout (Iowa City, IA, 1976), pp. 125–6.

45 Twain, *Adventures of Huckleberry Finn*, p. 155.

46 Mark Twain, *The Prince and the Pauper*, ed. Victor Fischer and Lin Salamo (Berkeley, CA, 1979), p. 90.

47 'Our Book Table', *Sacramento Daily Union*, 4 March 1882 (not in Budd).

48 Fears, *Mark Twain*, vol. I, p. 811.

49 See, for example, 'Life on the Mississippi', London *Morning Post*, 13 August 1883, p. 3 (not in Budd).

50 SLC to Charles C. Webster, 14 April 1884, *Letters to His Publishers, 1867–1894*, ed. Hamlin Hill (Berkeley, CA, 1967), p. 173.

51 Victor Fischer and Lin Salamo, 'Introduction', Mark Twain, *Adventures of Huckleberry Finn*, ed. Victor Fischer et al. (Berkeley, CA, 2003), pp. 705–6.

52 E. V. Lucas, 'E. V. Lucas and Twain at a 'Punch Dinner', *Bookman*, XXXVIII (1910), p. 116.

53 'The Adventures of Huckleberry Finn', London *Morning Post*, 3 February 1885, p. 3 (not in Budd).

6 The Wheel and the Wire

1   David H. Fears, *Mark Twain Day by Day* (Banks, OR, 2008–13), vol. I, p. 944.

2   Trebor Ohl, 'Mrs Florine Thayer McCray', *Queries*, V (1889), p. 143; Kevin J. Hayes, *The Two-wheeled World of George B. Thayer* (Lincoln, NE, 2015), pp. 22–7.

3   Kevin J. Hayes, 'Pedalling Preachers: Clergymen and the Acceptance of the Bicycle, 1881–1887', *Cycle History*, XX (2010), p. 20.

4   *Autobiography*, vol. II, p. 259.

5   'Wheel Notes', *St. Louis Globe-Democrat*, 19 May 1884, p. 9.

6   Fears, *Mark Twain Day by Day*, vol. I, p. 948.

7   'Echoes by the Way', *Publishers' Circular*, 10 January 1891, p. 17. For a variation, see Paul M. Zall, ed., *Mark Twain Laughing: Humorous Anecdotes by and about Samuel L. Clemens* (Knoxville, TN, 1985), no. 498.

8   Mark Twain, *What is Man? and Other Essays* (New York, 1917), p. 290.

9   Ibid., p. 296.

10 SLC to Charles L. Webster, 6 June 1884, in *Mark Twain, Business Man*, ed. Samuel Charles Webster (Boston, MA, 1846), p. 258.

11 *Notebooks*, vol. III, p. 55.

12 'Mark Twain', *Cleveland Herald*, 20 May 1884, p. 4.

13 Richard Garvey to SLC, 7 July 1884, in *Dear Mark Twain: Letters from His Readers*, ed. R. Kent Rasmussen (Berkeley, CA, 2013), p. 105; John Seelye, *Mark Twain in the Movies* (New York, 1977), pp. 10–13.

14 Henry Sturmey, *The 'Indispensable' Bicyclist's Handbook: A Complete Cyclopaedia upon the Subject of the Bicycle and Safety Bicycle, and Their Construction* (London, 1887), p. 82.

15 SLC to C.E.S. Wood, 24 July 1884, in Philip W. Leon, *Mark Twain and West Point* (Toronto, 1996), p. 232.

16 SLC to Joseph H. Twichell, 16 September 1884, in *The Letters of Mark Twain and Joseph Hopkins Twichell*, ed. Harold K. Bush, Steve Courtney and Peter Messent (Athens, GA, 2017), p. 133.

17 Mark Twain, 'Taming the Bicycle', folder no. Clemens 1.18, Archives and Special Collections, Vassar College Library, Poughkeepsie, NY.

18 Zack Furness, *One Less Car: Bicycling and the Politics of Automobility* (Philadelphia, PA, 2010), p. 16.

19 John Bird, 'Mark Twain on the Telephone: Love (and Hate) on the Line', *Mark Twain Annual*, VI (2008), p. 77.

20 SLC to Orion Clemens, 28 January 1878, *Mark Twain Project Online* (Berkeley, CA, 2007–16).

21 Kevin J. Hayes, 'Mark Twain Greets 1907', *Studies in American Humor*, new ser. III (1997), p. 92.

22 *Complete Interviews*, p. 573.

23 Mark Twain, 'The Loves of Alonzo Fitz Clarence and Rosannah Ethelton', *Atlantic*, XLI (1878), pp. 321, 324.

24 Gribben, vol. I, pp. 447–8.

25 Ibid., p. 124.

26 Garrison Keillor, 'Riverboat Rambler', *New York Times*, 19 December 2010, p. 6.

27 Gribben, vol. I, p. 362.

28 'Fred J. Hall Tells the Story of His Connection with Charles L. Webster & Co.', *Twainian*, November–December 1947, p. 2.

29 *Autobiography*, vol. I, p. 102.

30 Henry Nash Smith, 'Introduction', Mark Twain, *A Connecticut Yankee in King Arthur's Court*, ed. Bernard L. Stein (Berkeley, CA, 1979), pp. 10–11.

31 Ibid., p. 11.

32 Twain, *Connecticut Yankee*, pp. 130, 304.

33 Kevin J. Hayes, *A Journey through American Literature* (Oxford, 2012), p. 28.

34 Twain, *Connecticut Yankee*, p. 130.

35 Ibid., pp. 277–8.

36 Claude E. Shannon and Warren Weaver, *The Mathematical Theory of Communication* [1949] (Urbana, IL, 1964).

37 Twain, *Connecticut Yankee*, p. 276.

38 Ibid., pp. 425–6.

39 'In His New Book', *Wheel and Cycling Trade Review*, 28 February 1890, p. 21 (not in Budd).

40 Hayes, *Two-wheeled World*, p. 152.

41 'In His New Book', p. 21.

42 Hayes, *Two-wheeled World*, p. 154.

43 slc to Olivia L. Clemens, 19 April 1891, in *The Love Letters of Mark Twain*, ed. Dixon Wecter (New York, 1949), p. 259.

44 Gribben, vol. i, p. 58.

7 Journey to the End of the Night

1 slc to William Dean Howells, 24 August 1889, in *Mark Twain-Howells Letters*, ed. Henry Nash Smith and William M. Gibson (Cambridge, ma, 1960), vol. i, pp. 610–11.

2 Charles H. Gold, *'Hatching Ruin': or, Mark Twain's Road to Bankruptcy* (Columbia, mo, 2003), p. 45.

3 David H. Fears, *Mark Twain Day by Day* (Banks, or, 2008–13), vol. ii, pp. 520, 524.

4 'Fred J. Hall Tells the Story of His Connection with Charles L. Webster & Co.', *Twainian* (November–December 1947), pp. 1–3.

5 slc to Fred J. Hall, 3 February 1893, in *Letters to His Publishers, 1867–1894*, ed. Hamlin Hill (Berkeley, ca, 1967), p. 337.

6 slc to Fred J. Hall, 30 July 1893, in *Letters to His Publishers*, p. 354.

7 Hershel Parker, *Flawed Texts and Verbal Icons: Literary Authority in American Fiction* (Evanston, il, 1984), pp. 115–45.

8 Mark Twain, *The Tragedy of Pudd'nhead Wilson and the Comedy Those Extraordinary Twins* (Hartford, ct, 1894), p. 310; Richard Aldington, 'Mark Twain', *Spectator*, 29 November 1924, p. 830.

9 Twain, *Tragedy of Pudd'nhead Wilson*, p. 189.

10 George Orwell, *Complete Works* (London, 1986), vol. xvi, p. 5.

11 Mark Twain, *Following the Equator: A Journal around the World* (Hartford, ct, 1897), p. 129.

12 *Complete Interviews*, p. 227.

13 John Ruskin, *Sesame and Lilies* (London, 1865), p. 185.

14 Twain, *Following the Equator*, p. 345.

15 Ibid., p. 322.

16 Louis D. Rubin, Jr., 'Three Installments of Mark Twain', *Sewanee Review*, lxxviii (1970), p. 680.

17 *Mark Twain-Howells Letters*, vol. ii, p. 735n.

18 *Autobiography*, vol. i, p. 220.

19 Gribben, vol. ii, p. 523.

20 *Autobiography*, vol. II, pp. 113–14.
21 Ibid., vol. III, p. 213.
22 Laura Skandera Trombley, *Mark Twain in the Company of Women* (Philadelphia, PA, 1994), pp. 24–38.
23 Laura Skandera Trombley, *Mark Twain's Other Woman: The Hidden Story of His Final Years* (New York, 2010), pp. 61–2.

Bibliography

Scholarly Editions of Mark Twain's Writings

Anderson, Frederick, et al., eds, *Notebooks and Journals*, 3 vols
  (Berkeley, CA, 1975–9)
Baender, Paul, ed., *What Is Man? and Other Philosophical Writings*
  (Berkeley, CA, 1973)
Blair, Walter, ed., *Hannibal, Huck and Tom* (Berkeley, CA, 1969)
Branch, Edgar M., ed., *Clemens of the Call: Mark Twain in San Francisco*
  (Berkeley, CA, 1969)
Branch, Edgar Marquess, and Robert H. Hirst, eds, *Early Tales and Sketches,*
  2 vols (Berkeley, CA, 1979–81)
Budd, Louis J., ed., *Collected Tales, Sketches, Speeches, and Essays,* 2 vols
  (New York, 1992)
Fatout, Paul, ed., *Mark Twain Speaking* (Iowa City, IA, 1976)
Fischer, Victor, and Lin Salamo, eds, *Adventures of Huckleberry Finn*
  (Berkeley, CA, 2003)
—, eds, *The Prince and the Pauper* (Berkeley, CA, 1979)
Fishkin, Shelley Fisher, ed., *The Oxford Mark Twain*, 29 vols
  (Oxford, 1996)
Gerber, John C., Paul Baender and Terry Forkins, eds, *The Adventures
  of Tom Sawyer / Tom Sawyer Abroad / Tom Sawyer, Detective*
  (Berkeley, CA, 1980)
Gibson, William M., ed., *Mysterious Stranger Manuscripts* (Berkeley,
  CA, 1969)
McKeithan, Daniel Morley, ed., *Traveling with the Innocents Abroad:
  Mark Twain's Original Reports from Europe and the Holy Land*
  (Norman, OK, 1958)

Rogers, Franklin R., ed., *Satires and Burlesques* (Berkeley, CA, 1967)

Smith, Harriet Elinor, ed., *Autobiography of Mark Twain*, 3 vols
(Berkeley, CA, 2010–15)

—, and Edgar Marquess Branch, eds, *Roughing It* (Berkeley, CA, 1993)

Smith, Henry Nash, ed., *Mark Twain of the Enterprise: Newspaper Articles
and Other Documents, 1862–1864* (Berkeley, CA, 1957)

Stein, Bernard L., ed., *A Connecticut Yankee in King Arthur's Court*
(Berkeley, CA, 1979)

Tuckey, John S., ed., *Fables of Man* (Berkeley, CA, 1972)

—, ed., *Which Was the Dream? and Other Symbolic Writings of the Later
Years* (Berkeley, CA, 1967)

Scholarly Editions of Mark Twain's Letters

Branch, Edgar Marquess, et al., eds, *Letters*, 6 vols (Berkeley, CA,
1988–2002)

Cooley, John, ed., *Mark Twain's Aquarium: The Samuel Clemens Angelfish
Correspondence, 1905–1910* (Athens, GA, 1991)

Hill, Hamlin, ed., *Letters to His Publishers, 1867–1894* (Berkeley, CA, 1967)

Hornberger, Theodore, ed., *Mark Twain's Letters to Will Bowen:
'My First, & Oldest, & Dearest Friend'* (Austin, TX, 1941)

Leary, Lewis, ed., *Correspondence with Henry Huttleston Rogers, 1893–1909*
(Berkeley, CA, 1969)

—, ed., *Mark Twain's Letters to Mary* (New York, 1961)

Paine, Albert Bigelow, ed., *Mark Twain's Letters*, 2 vols (New York, 1917)

Smith, Henry Nash, and William M. Gibson, eds, *Mark Twain-Howells
Letters: The Correspondence of Samuel L. Clemens and William D.
Howells, 1872–1910*, 2 vols (Cambridge, MA, 1960)

Webster, Samuel Charles, ed., *Mark Twain, Business Man* (Boston,
MA, 1946)

Wecter, Dixon, ed., *The Love Letters of Mark Twain* (New York, 1949)

—, ed., *Mark Twain to Mrs Fairbanks* (San Marino, CA, 1949)

Reference Works

Budd, Louis J., ed., *Mark Twain: The Contemporary Reviews* (Cambridge, 1999)

Camfield, Gregg, *The Oxford Companion to Mark Twain* (Oxford, 2003)

Fears, David H., *Mark Twain Day by Day: An Annotated Chronology of the Life of Samuel L. Clemens*, 4 vols (Banks, OR, 2008–13)

Gribben, Alan, *Mark Twain's Library: A Reconstruction*, 2 vols (Boston, MA, 1980)

Johnson, Merle, *A Bibliography of the Works of Mark Twain, Samuel Langhorne Clemens: A List of First Editions in Book Form and of First Printings in Periodicals and Occasional Publications of His Varied Literary Activities* (New York, 1935)

LeMaster, J. R., and James D. Wilson, eds, *The Mark Twain Encyclopedia* (New York, 1993)

Machlis, Paul, and Ann Deborah Turner, *Union Catalog of Letters to Clemens* (Berkeley, CA, 1992)

Rasmussen, R. Kent, *Mark Twain A to Z: The Essential Reference to His Life and Writings* (New York, 1995)

Scharnhorst, Gary, ed., *Mark Twain: The Complete Interviews* (Tuscaloosa, AL, 2006)

Tenney, Thomas Asa, *Mark Twain: A Reference Guide* (Boston, MA, 1977)

Wilson, James D., *A Reader's Guide to the Short Stories of Mark Twain* (Boston, MA, 1987)

Zall, Paul M., ed., *Mark Twain Laughing: Humorous Anecdotes by and about Samuel L. Clemens* (Knoxville, TN, 1985)

Biographical, Critical and Historical Studies

Budd, Louis J., *Our Mark Twain: The Making of His Public Personality* (Philadelphia, PA, 1983)

Coulombe, Joseph L., *Mark Twain and the American West* (Columbia, NY, 2003)

Cox, James M., *Mark Twain: The Fate of Humor* (Princeton, NJ, 1966)

Doyno, Victor, *Writing Huck Finn: Mark Twain's Creative Process* (Philadelphia, PA, 1991)

Emerson, Everett H., *Mark Twain: A Literary Life* (Philadelphia, PA, 2000)

Fulton, Joe B., *Mark Twain in the Margins: The Quarry Farm Marginalia and A Connecticut Yankee in King Arthur's Court* (Tuscaloosa, AL, 2000)

Ganzel, Dewey, *Mark Twain Abroad: The Cruise of the Quaker City* (Chicago, IL, 1968)

Gibson, William M., *The Art of Mark Twain* (New York, 1976)

Hill, Hamlin, *Mark Twain: God's Fool* (New York, 1973)

Kaplan, Juston, *Mr Clemens and Mark Twain: A Biography* (New York, 1966)

Leary, Lewis, *Mark Twain* (Minneapolis, MN, 1960)

Melton, Jeffrey Alan, *Mark Twain, Travel Books, and Tourism: The Tide of a Great Popular Movement* (Tuscaloosa, AL, 2002)

Messent, Peter B., *The Cambridge Introduction to Mark Twain* (Cambridge, 2007)

Michelson, Bruce, *Mark Twain on the Loose: A Comic Writer and the American Self* (Amherst, MA, 1995)

Parker, Hershel, *Flawed Texts and Verbal Icons: Literary Authority in American Fiction* (Evanston, IL, 1984)

Quirk, Tom, *Coming to Grips with Huckleberry Finn: Essays on a Book, a Boy, and a Man* (Columbia, MO, 1993)

Robinson, Forrest G., ed., *The Cambridge Companion to Mark Twain* (Cambridge, 1995)

—, *In Bad Faith: The Dynamics of Deception in Mark Twain's America* (Cambridge, MA, 1986)

Sattelmeyer, Robert, and J. Donald Crowley, eds, *One Hundred Years of Huckleberry Finn: The Boy, His Book, and American Culture: Centennial Essays* (Columbia, NY, 1985)

Seelye, John, *Mark Twain in the Movies: A Meditation with Pictures* (New York, 1977)

—, *The True Adventures of Huckleberry Finn* (Evanston, IL, 1970)

Shillingsburg, Miriam Jones, *At Home Abroad: Mark Twain in Australasia* (Jackson, MS, 1988)

Smith, Henry Nash, *Mark Twain: The Development of a Writer* (Cambridge, MA, 1962)

—, *Mark Twain's Fable of Progress: Political and Economic Ideas in A Connecticut Yankee* (New Brunswick, NJ, 1964)

Steinbrink, Jeffrey, *Getting to Be Mark Twain* (Berkeley, CA, 1991)

Trombley, Laura E. Skandera, *Mark Twain in the Company of Women* (Philadelphia, PA, 1994)

—, *Mark Twain's Other Woman: The Hidden Story of His Final Years* (New York, 2010)

Wecter, Dixon, *Sam Clemens of Hannibal* (Boston, MA, 1952)

Acknowledgements

Beneath a striped circus canopy I first encountered Mark Twain. It was the late 1960s, and Mom and Dad – who belong in every list of acknowledgements – took me to Toledo's annual outdoor book fair. Several canopies had been erected, and they sheltered dozens of folding tables holding thousands of books, all displayed with their spines facing up. I bought my first copy of *Tom Sawyer* at that book fair. In one form or another Mark Twain has re-entered my life practically every decade since.

My college professors deserve a paragraph of their own in these acknowledgements. As an undergraduate at the University of Toledo in the late 1970s, I had the good fortune to take Wallace Martin's seminar on literary criticism. Professor Martin used *Huckleberry Finn* as an extended example, applying several different critical approaches to illustrate the book's narrative complexity and theory's interpretive possibilities. As a graduate student at the University of Delaware in the late 1980s, I read *Pudd'nhead Wilson* in Hershel Parker's seminar on textual editing. A real eye-opener, Parker's seminar let me know that all those critical theories Martin taught me were problematic if they had been based on flawed texts.

After becoming a professor myself, I had the opportunity to teach a summer Mark Twain seminar during the mid-1990s. The first Mark Twain seminar I taught coincided with the Great Flood of 1993. Nightly news stories about the Mississippi flood supplemented our daily discussions of Twain's world. My students deserve acknowledgement for our lively classroom discussions. Once I submitted my manuscript for *Herman Melville*, an earlier volume in Reaktion's Critical Lives series, publisher Michael Leaman asked if I would like to write a Mark Twain volume for the series. Happy for the opportunity to contribute another volume to this outstanding series, I gratefully accepted his offer. Teaching Mark

Twain, it turned out, had been excellent preparation for writing about Mark Twain, though I have had to brush up my Twain scholarship.

Perhaps no place has been more useful (or more pleasant) to help me brush up my scholarship than Quarry Farm, where Twain spent his summers and wrote his finest works. Quarry Farm has since become the Elmira College Center for Mark Twain Studies. I would like to thank Joseph Lemak, Director of the Center for Mark Twain Studies, for offering me a fellowship to visit the centre and working out all the logistics; caretaker Steve Webb for his hospitality while my wife Myung-Sook and I stayed at Quarry Farm; Matt Seybold for all the ideas he shared over shepherd's pie and pints of stout at Horigan's Tavern; and Nathaniel Ball, Director of the Mark Twain Archive, Gannett-Tripp Library, Elmira College, who guided me through its collections of manuscripts and photographs.

Other individuals and institutions also deserve thanks: Sierra Dixon, Connecticut Historical Society; Megan Goins-Diouf, The Center for Archival Collections, Jerome Library, Bowling Green State University; and Dean Rogers, Archives and Special Collections, Vassar College Library. The librarians at the Sanger Branch of the Toledo Lucas County Public Library also deserve acknowledgement. Researching this book, I made numerous requests from OhioLink, the statewide consortium of academic libraries, which the Sanger librarians filled with kindness and expedience. As always, I thank Myung-Sook, whose unwavering enthusiasm and curiosity have encouraged me to further my studies of literature and life.

Photo Acknowledgements

The author and the publishers wish to express their thanks to the below sources of illustrative material and /or permission to reproduce it.

Denison University Library, Granville, OH: pp. 23, 76, 77, 78, 79, 80, 83, 85; Collection of Kevin J. Hayes, Toledo, OH: pp. 142, 147; Library of Congress, Prints and Photographs Division, Washington, DC: pp. 19 (LG-DIG-ds-04477), 20 (LC-USZ62-74794), 30 (LC-DIG-pga-00099), 31 (LC-USZC4-3168), 34 (LC-DIG-pga-03028), 43 (LC-DIG-pga-01999), 44 (LC-DIG-pga-03398), 51 (LC-DIG-pga-01018), 54 (LC-DIG-ds-04486), 59 (HABS CAL,55-JACHI,1-4), 60 (LC-DIG-highsm-23560), 96 (LC-DIG-cwpbh-00450), 110 (HABS CONN, 2-HARF, 16-13), 113 (HABS CONN, 2-HARF, 16-89), 118 (LC-USZ62-98767), 139 (LC-USZ62-110720), 152 (LC-DIG-var-0609), 157 (LC-DIG-ds-04511), 166 (LC-USZ62-60535); The Ohio State University Library, Columbus, OH: p. 82; Mark Twain Archive, Elmira College, Elmira, NY: pp. 6, 99, 104, 105, 106, 107, 109, 165; Mark Twain Archive, Elmira College, Elmira, NY and Kevin MacDonnell, Austin, TX: p. 158.